THE NONPROFIT CRISIS

THE NONPROFIT CRISIS

Leadership Through the Culture Wars

Greg Berman

OXFORD
UNIVERSITY PRESS

Oxford University Press is a department of the University of Oxford. It furthers the University's objective of excellence in research, scholarship, and education by publishing worldwide. Oxford is a registered trade mark of Oxford University Press in the UK and in certain other countries.

Published in the United States of America by Oxford University Press
198 Madison Avenue, New York, NY 10016, United States of America.

CIP data is on file at the Library of Congress

ISBN 9780197786307
ISBN 9780197786291 (hbk.)

DOI: 10.1093/oso/9780197786291.001.0001

Paperback printed by Integrated Books International, United States of America
Hardback printed by Bridgeport National Bindery, Inc., United States of America

The manufacturer's authorized representative in the EU for product safety is Oxford University Press España S.A., Parque Empresarial San Fernando de Henares, Avenida de Castilla, 2—28830 Madrid (www.oup.es/en or product.safety@oup.com). OUP España S.A. also acts as importer into Spain of products made by the manufacturer.

For Mitzi and Allan

As far as I can make out, a conservative temperament has something to do with a deep understanding of the inherent value of the world, and its vulnerable and precarious nature. It is suspicious of the impulse to tear things down, dismantle things, cancel things, burn things to the ground, rather it's more naturally inclined toward cautious, incremental change, because we need to be careful with the world. The conservative understands about loss and about grief. I'm certainly open to new things, but with an appreciation of what has gone before and a melancholy understanding that it is a lot easier to tear things down than to build them back up. But, at the end of the day, I think conservatism is an aspiration, it is something we should strive for—a society that works well enough that it is worth conserving. I don't think we are there yet, there are things yet left to reform, of course, but I think we are generally moving in the right direction.

—Nick Cave

CONTENTS

Acknowledgments *ix*

PART I
A WORLD OF PAIN

Introduction: Nonprofits Under Attack 3

1. Fault Lines 21

2. The Generational Divide 35

3. Polarization 52

4. The Rise and Fall (and Rise Again?) of DEI 69

PART II

A WAY THROUGH

5. Good Stewardship 93

6. Who Decides? 106

7. The Nonprofit Mentoring Crisis 118

8. Mission Creep 131

9. Leadership Transition 144

Conclusion: The Challenge of Accountability 160

Epilogue: The Return of Trump 177

Endnotes *184*
Index *201*

ACKNOWLEDGMENTS

I stepped down from running the Center for Court Innovation, a large criminal-justice reform nonprofit in New York City, in 2020. My final day was March 13, the first day that the Covid lockdown really went into effect. I didn't go into work on my last day. No cake. No goodbyes. I was just gone.

The date of my departure was just a matter of chance—my last day had been arranged months in advance. But the timing was fortuitous, at least in certain respects.

In the days leading up to my departure, as I readied myself to leave a job that I loved, I feared that I would find myself on the outside looking in, with my face pressed up against the glass, watching as everyone continued the party without me. I think this fear is a big reason why many nonprofit executive directors end up overstaying their welcome. (More on this in Chapter 9.)

The Covid lockdown meant that didn't happen. Immediately, everything changed. There was no party. Everyone was at home, just like me. So, in many respects, Covid made my transition away from the Center for Court Innovation much easier.

But if my life was going pretty well, I couldn't help but notice that this wasn't the case for many of my former peers.

Much of my social circle is composed of nonprofit leaders. In addition, in 2020, I began a three-year run of interviewing nonprofit executives and writing up the results in a regular column for *City & State* and *New York Nonprofit Media*. As a result, almost every week, I was talking to nonprofit executives. The stories I heard had a lot in common—everyone seemed to be having a hard time.

There were good reasons for their struggles. Many were working from their closets or their bathrooms, conducting Zoom meetings while their children played or went to school on the other side of the door. No one really knew how to adapt their operations to lockdown; everyone was just kind of making things up as they went along.

There was also a lot of pain and anger in the air. Many nonprofit staffers were unhappy—and they were not shy about letting the world know about it. It was a presidential election year and the prospect of another term in office for Donald Trump was generating high volumes of political engagement, both for and against. The death of George Floyd in Minneapolis kicked emotions up to another level. Protests in the streets were quickly followed by demands for change within many nonprofit organizations. The leaders of those organizations strained to keep up with it all.

I watched all of this playing out from the comforts of my living room. I didn't have to wrestle with staff discontent or the complicated politics of the moment. I was no longer in the game.

Still, I empathized with those who were. More or less overnight, the job of nonprofit leader had become next to impossible. I watched in dismay as many nonprofit agencies that I admired started to wobble. Some all but collapsed.

This seemed to me an important development. I believe that nonprofits are essential to the health of our democracy. Nobody wins when nonprofits aren't able to do their jobs effectively.

This book is my effort to explain what has happened to American nonprofits in recent years and why it matters—and to try to sketch how it might be prevented from happening again.

I wrote most of this book in 2024 prior to Donald Trump's victory in that year's presidential election. I send it out into the world now with some trepidation. As I detail in the Epilogue, just a single week into his second term, Trump has already signaled an urge for disruption and retribution that could have a massive impact on American nonprofits. By the time this book hits the shelves, the playing field could look very different. Still, the fundamental challenge I have outlined in these pages—the need to reverse an alarming erosion of public trust in nonprofits—isn't going anywhere. Indeed, it is just as likely to get worse as it is to get better unless nonprofits make some significant changes.

***

My introduction to nonprofit management came not long after I moved to New York in 1992. I was in my mid-twenties and I was trying to find my place in the world. By chance, I stumbled into a world of smart and sophisticated nonprofits, many of which were working to bring New York City back to health after several challenging decades. After years of searching, I had found my people.

My original connection to this world was John Feinblatt. As I describe in Chapter 7, I will always owe a great debt to John for giving me my big professional break and mentoring me at a formative stage in my development.

I was part of the founding team that created the Center for Court Innovation (now the Center for Justice Innovation) and I served as its executive director for nearly 20 years. Almost everything I know about nonprofits comes from my direct experience helping to build the Center. I was there when the organization started and by the time I left, it had a budget of nearly $80 million. I have sprinkled a few stories from my days at the Center throughout this manuscript, in an effort to provide a little texture and to offer readers a better sense of where I'm coming from.

The Center provided me with a base of operations for some very important changes in my life—getting married, buying a home, and having children, to name a few. It also introduced me to a remarkable set of colleagues. Traces of many of them can be found in these pages. My successor as the executive director of the Center, Courtney Bryan, is high on this list. I am lucky to have her as a friend, and I have learned a lot from watching her work and seeing the Center grow under her leadership.

Since leaving the Center for Court Innovation, I have devoted the lion's share of my time to helping to create a policy journal dedicated to advancing new thinking about how to improve life in New York and other cities. I am grateful to Liz Glazer for coming up with the idea for *Vital City* and for asking me to come along for the ride. I'm enormously proud of the work we have done together, along with managing editor Josh Greenman and the rest of our small team.

In addition to *Vital City*, the last several years of my life have been shaped by my engagement with The Harry Frank Guggenheim Foundation. Dan Wilhelm welcomed me to the Foundation as a fellow back in 2020. My affiliation with the Foundation has given me the space to think about a range of different topics and an excuse to talk with dozens of prominent thinkers and scholars.

For this, as well as his willingness to be a sounding board and a friend, I will always be grateful to Dan.

A few other acknowledgments:

This book was originally conceived as a joint project with my friend Aubrey Fox. We had already written two books together—*Gradual: The Case for Incremental Change in a Radical Age* and *Trial & Error in Criminal Justice Reform: Learning From Failure*—and we were eager to make it a trilogy. Unfortunately, Aubrey has a demanding day job as the executive director of New York City's Criminal Justice Agency, so he ended up not being able to find the necessary time to devote to this project. Nevertheless, he made a significant contribution, helping to frame the structure of this book, working on a proposal to Oxford University Press, and offering valuable feedback along the way. I am grateful for his insight and his friendship and look forward to working with him again in the future.

Thanks to *City & State*'s Tom Allon for allowing me to write a regular column on nonprofit leadership for three years. Thanks to Ralph Ortega for his kindness and generosity as an editor.

Thanks to Niko Pfund at Oxford University Press for his friendship and support of this book as well as *Gradual*. Thanks to David McBride for his deft editorial stewardship.

I have talked with many current and former nonprofit leaders in putting this book together. Some of them appear by name in these pages. Others asked to be granted anonymity. In either case, I thank them for their time and willingness to share their observations.

In recent years, I have also talked about this project in broad strokes with a number of friends and colleagues. For their insight, I thank: Julian Adler, Amy Barasch, Mischael Cetoute, Carolyn Volpe Cunningham, Laurel Dumont, Meg Egan, Amy Ellenbogen,

Beth Goldman, Eric Lee, Rich Leimsider, Scott Millstein, Justine Olderman, Michele Sviridoff, Mindy Tarlow, and Jeff Wetzler. Special thanks to those who read and commented on portions of the manuscript: Liberty Aldrich, Courtney Bryan, John Maki, Kevin Ring, Daniel Stid, Chris Watler, and Dan Wilhelm.

I thank John Bostwick and Bill McConagha for their regular, sanity-preserving correspondence with me.

Finally, thanks to my family of origin—Allan, Michele, and M.J.—for their love, support, and forbearance. Thanks to my daughters, Hannah and Milly, for inspiring me with their creativity. And thanks most of all to my wife, Carolyn Vellenga Berman, for being a thought partner, co-conspirator, muse, and so much more.

PART I

A WORLD OF PAIN

Nonprofits Under Attack

In 1831, a minor French government functionary named Alexis de Tocqueville arrived in the United States. His assignment was to study the American prison system. He could read English, but he was not a fluent speaker. He was all of 26 years old.

No one could have predicted that, at the end of his sojourn, Tocqueville would produce an enduring masterpiece of political science that is still being studied nearly 200 years later. But that's exactly what he did.

Over the course of a 10-month visit, Tocqueville conducted library research and numerous interviews with both prominent and ordinary Americans. His curiosity would end up taking him far beyond his assigned topic to incorporate a wide-ranging investigation of American politics, social life, race relations, and more.

One of Tocqueville's signal intellectual contributions in *Democracy in America* was to highlight the importance of what he called "public associations" to the vitality of the American project:

> Americans of all ages, all conditions, and all dispositions, constantly form associations . . . [of a thousand] kinds—religious, moral, serious, futile, extensive or restricted, enormous or diminutive. The Americans make associations to give entertainments, to found establishments for education, to build inns,

> to construct churches, to diffuse books, to send missionaries to the antipodes; and in this manner they found hospitals, prisons, and schools. If it be proposed to advance some truth, or to foster some feeling by the encouragement of a great example, they form a society. Wherever, at the head of some new undertaking, you see the government in France, or a man of rank in England, in the United States you will be sure to find an association.[1]

Tocqueville saw these public associations as important democratic institutions, taking up a variety of tasks that government never would and offering ordinary citizens a kind of collective power that they could never achieve individually.

Much of what Tocqueville called associations we would today call nonprofit organizations.[2]

As Tocqueville observed, the nonprofit sector is one of the pillars of American society. Each and every day, Americans turn to nonprofits for a staggering variety of purposes. Nonprofits are responsible for educating our children, healing the sick, and clothing the indigent. But this just scratches the surface. Nonprofits provide jobs to the formerly incarcerated, conduct research into climate change, and help young people learn to play sports. They deliver legal services to immigrants, offer loans to homeowners, and take care of our pets. The list goes on and on.

According to the National Center for Charitable Statistics, approximately 1.5 million nonprofits are registered with the Internal Revenue Service. The nonprofit sector contributed more than $1 trillion to the American economy in 2016.[3] By the end of that year, the nonprofit sector was the third-largest employer in the country.[4]

But numbers don't adequately convey the extent to which the nonprofit sector functions as the warp and woof of American society. According to Lester Salamon, editor of *The State of Nonprofit America*, "The nonprofit sector is one of the most important components of American life, but it is also one of the least understood."[5]

A WALK THROUGH THE *TIMES*

If you want to wrap your arms around the scope and importance of the nonprofit sector in today's America—but unlike Alexis de Tocqueville, you don't have 10 months to spare—a good place to start is an edition of the *New York Times*.

At first glance, this might seem an odd choice. After all, there is no "Nonprofit" section of the *Times*, the way there is a daily "Business" section. On an average day, the words "nonprofit" may not even appear in the paper. Nonetheless, if you know where and how to look, almost every edition of the *Times* offers testimony to the importance of nonprofit organizations.

Flip open your paper to the Arts section, for example. (Or toggle your mouse, as the case may be.) There you will find reviews of the latest movies, shows, and museum exhibits. Perhaps you will see appraisals of plays performed at Lincoln Center, Brooklyn Academy of Music, or the New York Shakespeare Festival—all nonprofits. *Hamilton*, one of the biggest Broadway hits of the past decade, began its run in a nonprofit theater (The Public). All told, it is estimated that not-for-profit theaters contributed nearly $2.1 billion to the U.S. economy and attracted 23 million attendees in 2020.[6]

Most Hollywood films are produced by for-profit companies, of course. Still, nonprofits are an integral part of the movie business, from the Oscars (The Academy of Motion Picture Arts & Sciences) to the rating system (the Motion Picture Association) to the film festival circuit (many prominent film festivals, like Sundance and Tribeca, are organized by nonprofits).

Or maybe instead of a movie you prefer to attend an art exhibition. Almost all of New York City's major museums are nonprofit institutions. The Met, MoMA, the Whitney, the Guggenheim, the Frick . . . all nonprofits. Indeed, it is impossible to imagine cultural life in the United States without the nonprofit sector. We depend on nonprofits to nurture and subsidize our writers, artists, and musicians as they develop. And nonprofits like the Smithsonian Institution are essential to preserving our cultural heritage for future generations.

As an unexpected chronicler of nonprofit activity, the Arts section is rivaled by the Sports section. To be sure, much of the sports world is a tale of capitalism run amuck—millionaire athletes plying their trade for billionaire sports-team owners pursuing ever richer contracts from multinational broadcasting corporations. But here too, some of the most important players in the game turn out to be nonprofit institutions. The National College Athletic Association is responsible for organizing March Madness and the College Football Championship. The International Olympic Committee puts on the Olympics. FIFA manages the World Cup. All are nonprofit organizations. Perhaps most shockingly of all, the National Football League—arguably the embodiment of unbridled athletic avarice—was, up until relatively recently, a nonprofit organization.[7]

But to really witness the power and influence of nonprofit organizations, the best place to turn is the front section of the *New York Times,* where the hard news resides. It is true that the primary actors in the A section tend to be government officials of one kind or another—the President, Congress, and so on. But what they are discussing and doing has been profoundly shaped by the nonprofit community. Try to imagine the abortion debate without Planned Parenthood or the National Right to Life Committee. Or the gun control conversation without the National Rifle Association and Everytown for Gun Safety. Or free speech controversies without the American Civil Liberties Union. Or artificial intelligence discussions without OpenAI.

The legislative platforms of the Democratic and Republican parties are not developed in a vacuum. A swarm of nonprofit activist groups and think tanks are working every day to shape the public policy agenda. Many of them will be recognizable names to anyone who has ever read a newspaper—the Heritage Foundation, Brookings Institution, Sierra Club, Greenpeace, Human Rights Watch, NAACP, Children's Defense Fund, and many, many more.

But nonprofits aren't just drafting policy papers and pressing the flesh on Capitol Hill—they are essential to almost any effort to get things done in the United States. The fight against cancer would not be possible without the American Cancer Society, the Mayo Clinic, and hundreds of hospitals around the country. The effort to care for the less fortunate could not advance without the Salvation Army, Goodwill, and the Red Cross. The schooling of American children is dependent not just on Harvard and 1,600 other private colleges and universities, but on the 34,000 private and religious secondary schools that educate 5.7 million students each year.

I could go on, but you get the point. For generations, the nonprofit sector was one of the underappreciated strengths of the United States, an invisible but essential emollient that helped to oil the great American machine. According to author Freddie de-Boer, the nonprofit sector is "an immensely influential part of our society, yet public interest in it appears low. Nonprofits play a disproportionate role in our political apparatus, our educational systems, and our basic civic functioning, but most Americans putter along without pausing to think too much about them."[8]

Thankfully, in recent years, this has begun to change. A growing number of prominent commentators on both the right and the left are starting to appreciate the importance of American nonprofits. Unfortunately, they have come not to praise the sector, but to bury it.

"THE NONPROFIT INDUSTRIAL COMPLEX"

In 1961, President Dwight Eisenhower warned Americans of the growing threat posed by the "military industrial complex," a sprawling network of influential businesses, organizations, and politicians that sought to expand military spending regardless of whether those expenditures were in the best interests of the country. In the years since 1961, the "-industrial complex" formulation has been used to describe a variety of situations where a nefarious group of actors seeks to build their own profits at the expense of the greater good—see, for example, the "prison industrial complex."

Over the past 20 years or so, a growing chorus of radical critics has begun to argue that the nonprofit sector amounts to a self-serving industrial complex. For example, in 2004, a group of activists known as INCITE! convened a gathering that eventually turned into an anthology titled *The Revolution Will Not Be Funded: Beyond the Non-Profit Industrial Complex.*[9]

INCITE! and the nonprofit detractors who have followed in their wake offer a fundamental critique of the American nonprofit model. Back in 1831, Tocqueville had suggested that American public associations were performing work independent of government and were harnessing the power of the people. Opponents of the nonprofit industrial complex suggest that today's American charities are achieving neither of these goals.

The argument goes something like this: American nonprofits often call themselves "the independent sector," but this is a misnomer at best and subterfuge at worst. Indeed, many nonprofit organizations are deeply intertwined with the state, relying upon government grants to keep the lights on. Even when nonprofits don't depend on government revenues, their activities are often influenced by another set of powerful purse strings—money that comes from rich people or corporations or wealthy foundations.

As anyone who has worked in a nonprofit can attest, where the money comes from does shape and constrain what a nonprofit does. Sometimes this is explicit—many grants come with clearly defined rules and restrictions that must be obeyed in order for the money to be paid. More often, the influence that funders exert on nonprofits is of a subtle variety. To get money from a funder, you have to be able to speak their language, both literally and metaphorically. This typically means not challenging their values or assumptions. To truly play the game at the highest level, raising millions from government and foundations, requires a high degree of professionalization from nonprofits, who must employ lawyers and accountants and other fancy specialists if they are to meet the demands for reporting from government bureaucrats and philanthropic executives.

To radical critics, all of this means that nonprofits are prevented from pursuing a truly transformational social change agenda, which might entail overthrowing capitalism and replacing the government with something better. At the same time, nonprofits are draining resources and energy away from the public sector, in the process weakening government and reducing public support for the expansion of the welfare state.

The most cynical of nonprofit critics argue that nonprofit organizations are essentially false flag operations—that they aren't really interested in ending homelessness or addiction or any other social problem. Indeed, their livelihood depends upon the continued existence of these problems. Instead of solving the problems that they were ostensibly created to address, nonprofits are mostly in the business of self-perpetuation and lining the pockets of their executives, many of whom earn surprisingly large salaries.

This kind of critical appraisal of the nonprofit sector was once a fringe phenomenon, the province of radical organizers with little audience or influence. But variations on this theme have begun to infiltrate more mainstream venues. In a widely shared *New York Times* op-ed, Peter Buffet (the son of fabled investor Warren Buffet) called out "philanthropic colonialism" and "conscience laundering" that conspire to keep the "existing structure of inequality in place."[10]

In a similar vein, Anand Giridharadas's popular 2018 book, *Winners Take All: The Elite Charade of Changing the World*, exposed the contradictions of well-heeled advocates for social justice. While Giridharadas's primary targets were business elites, his charge—that many who "believe they are changing the world" are, in reality, "protecting a system that is at the root of the problems they wish to solve"—reiterates the basic argument against the nonprofit industrial complex.[11] Even *Teen Vogue* got into the act, asking, "If the issues we face are rooted in systems of government oppression and capitalism, how can we expect nonprofits, which are complicit in the same systems, to solve them?"[12]

For some left-wing critics, the nonprofit sector isn't a bunch of well-meaning do-gooders trying desperately to make the world a better place—it's another enemy to be vanquished.

O'SULLIVAN'S FIRST LAW

John O'Sullivan is a controversial British conservative. After working in government (as a speechwriter for Margaret Thatcher) and journalism (as an editor for the *National Review*), O'Sullivan now runs a think tank called the Danube Institute, which has been accused of serving as an apologist for Viktor Orbán's populist authoritarianism in Hungary. But O'Sullivan is perhaps best known for a single line he wrote back in 1989: "All organizations that are not actually right-wing will over time become left-wing."[13] This is O'Sullivan's First Law.

The Ford Foundation is perhaps the paradigmatic example of O'Sullivan's Law in practice. Founded in 1936 by Edsel Ford, the son of Henry Ford and the president of the Ford Motor Company, the Ford Foundation was originally headquartered in Michigan and supported local projects, including museums and hospitals. As the years went by, things changed. Edsel Ford passed away. The foundation moved to New York and divested itself of Ford Motors stock. A new, broader mission was announced that included grantmaking around the world. The Ford family drifted away from the foundation, capped in 1977 when Henry Ford II stepped down as a trustee. In a stinging resignation letter, Ford issued a host of complaints, including that the staff of the foundation failed to appreciate the capitalist system that was the source of the money the foundation gave away. Today, the Ford Foundation makes its left-wing orientation explicit, proudly declaring on its website: "We are disrupting systems to advance social justice."[14]

Conservative critiques of nonprofit America tend to be variations on O'Sullivan's First Law. (It is worth noting here that conservative institutions are hardly immune to rot over time. In recent years, many organizations that used to be viewed as thoughtful intellectual voices have been captured by the populist wing of the conservative movement. The Heritage Foundation's controversial Project 2025 is a case in point. Ideological drift would appear to be an equal opportunity problem.)

Nevertheless, conservatives believe, with some justification, that many, if not most, nonprofits are left-leaning institutions. This belief has been around for a while. Indeed, it helped to spark a wave of institution building in the 1970s, as conservative activists and funders sought to create a rival nonprofit infrastructure that would support the advancement of free markets and traditional social values.

There are other conservative criticisms of nonprofits, to be sure, including the accusation that they are inefficient, unaccountable, and should operate more like businesses, but at the root is the concern that nonprofits have a left-wing bias that is out of step with mainstream America.

In recent years, the force of this belief has only intensified. As the apparatus of the Democratic Party has gotten weaker, the power of left-leaning nonprofit organizations has become more and more apparent. In their book *Where Have All the Democrats Gone?*, John B. Judis and Ruy Teixeira argue that there is now a "shadow party" comprised of "organizations like the American Civil Liberties Union, the Sunrise Movement, Planned Parenthood, and Black Lives Matter, publications such as the *New York*

Times, MSNBC, and *Vox*, foundations like Ford and Open Society, and think tanks like the Center for American Progress."[15] Judis and Teixeira believe that these groups, which are largely staffed by college-educated elites, have heavily influenced the direction of the Democratic Party for the worse.

This analysis is shared by Michael Lind, a professor and co-founder of the New America think tank.[16] According to Lind,

> Intellectual life on the American center-left is dead. Debate has been replaced by compulsory assent and ideas have been replaced by slogans that can be recited but not questioned: Black Lives Matter, Green Transition, Trans Women Are Women, 1619, Defund the Police. The space to the left-of-center that was once filled with magazines and organizations devoted to what Diana Trilling called the "life of significant contention" is now filled by the ritualized gobbledygook of foundation-funded single-issue nonprofits like a pond choked by weeds. Having crowded out dissent and debate, the nonprofit industrial complex—Progressivism, Inc.—taints the Democratic Party by association with its bizarre obsessions and contributes to Democratic electoral defeats.

What Lind labels "ritualized gobbledygook," other, sharper-elbowed observers have called "wokeness"—a constellation of radical ideas about identity that are often expressed in jargon imported from academia (e.g., "decolonization," "intersectionality," "equity"). Concerns about the promulgation of these ideas have animated conservative institutions like the Manhattan Institute and the *Wall Street Journal* editorial page to launch a series of attacks against nonprofit organizations and foundations in recent years.

For some right-wing critics, the nonprofit sector isn't a bunch of well-meaning do-gooders trying desperately to make the world a better place—it's another enemy to be vanquished.

DECLINING PUBLIC TRUST

So nonprofit organizations have been under siege from both the left and the right, a phenomenon that has been abetted in recent years by the spread of social media, which offers anyone with a strong opinion a megaphone that they can use to broadcast their concerns to the world. While the impact of all this discourse is likely to be negligible on any individual organization, there are signs that it is beginning to have an effect on the sector as a whole.

Most Americans don't think about nonprofits very much. But those that do tend to think reasonably well of the sector, particularly when compared to other American institutions. That makes sense: nonprofits are explicitly chartered to advance the public good. Popular opinion about them should be less conflicted than it is toward institutions—like Congress, the Supreme Court, and the criminal justice system—that, by their nature, spark more ambivalent reactions.

But there are ominous signs that public trust in nonprofit America is ebbing. For the past four years, the Independent Sector, a membership organization of nonprofits and foundations, has conducted a national survey to document the state of trust in the sector. The findings of the most recent survey (2023) are telling:

- Nonprofits were trusted by a majority of respondents, but just barely (52%). Nonprofits did rank significantly higher than such institutions as philanthropy (34%), corporations (26%), and the news media (24%).

- Trust in nonprofits has fallen each year that the Independent Sector has conducted its survey. The decline from 2022 to 2023 (4 percentage points) was the largest year-to-year change in any institution tested.
- Trust in nonprofits is highly variable, depending upon the nature of the organization. For example, 68% of respondents expressed high trust in human service agencies, compared to 49% expressing support in civil rights organizations.
- Political partisanship plays a role in determining trust, with wide variations in how Democrats and Republicans view nonprofits. For example, Republicans are much more likely to trust places of worship (62%) than they are environmental advocacy organizations (40%).[17]

It might be tempting for nonprofits to view the results of this survey as no big deal—after all, the sector does do better than most other institutions. But the fact that nearly half of respondents do not express trust in nonprofits should be viewed as a flashing warning sign. A 2022 Morning Consult poll offers more ominous tidings, documenting trust in nonprofits declining with each passing generation: only 46% of Gen Z adults expressed trust in nonprofits compared with 67% of baby boomers.[18] Nonprofits are on the brink.

What is to be done? How can nonprofit leaders adapt to the new realities confronting them? And in an era of public disenchantment with institutions of all kinds, is it possible to bolster trust in America's nonprofit organizations?

These are the questions that animate this book.

A FORCE FOR GOOD?

To put my cards on the table: I believe that the nonprofit sector, by and large, is a force for good in the world. I do not subscribe to either the left- or the right-wing critiques of nonprofit America—at least not in whole. Nonprofit organizations are not standing in the way of the revolution or undermining the health of American government. Nor are they dangers to the populace, deliberately undermining American values.

Having said that, there are elements of truth to both the left- and right-wing critiques of the sector. And if nonprofits do not listen carefully to these critical assessments, and respond accordingly, they will continue to hemorrhage public support. I want to avoid this fate.

I have written this book out of a sense of deep concern for the health of American nonprofit organizations. The state of the nonprofit sector should be a priority for all Americans. After all, the strength of our nonprofit sector is one of the things that distinguishes the United States from all other countries. The sector is essential to our civic life. We need our social service agencies and sense-making organizations to function to the best of their abilities in order for American democracy to thrive.

This book is primarily concerned with what nonprofit leaders can and should do. While leadership is my emphasis, this is not intended to be a self-help book or a guide to management. And while I will discuss the impact of our political discourse on nonprofits, this book is not a culture-war screed. Rather, it is an effort to paint a detailed picture of life within American nonprofit institutions over the past few years—and to articulate what good nonprofit leadership looks like given the multi-faceted challenges these are organizations are currently facing.

The nonprofit sector is so large and so diverse that it is difficult to write or think about it in a coherent way. Harvard, with its $50 billion endowment that is larger than the GDP of dozens of countries, is a nonprofit. So is your local block association with no employees and no office space. It is fair to ask whether Harvard and the block association have anything in common beyond their tax-exempt status.

While I will use the term "nonprofit" throughout this book, I will often be talking about a certain kind of nonprofit: those that provide human services. This includes organizations that are seeking to solve social problems like homelessness, poverty, and child abuse. These groups are offering childcare, building housing, and providing drug treatment, among many other services. While they are just one part of a vast constellation of nonprofits, they are particularly important because they are interacting with millions of Americans every day and they are often prominent institutions in local communities. Indeed, some critics have argued that these kinds of nonprofits amount to a "permanent government" in many cities.

This book focuses on the trials presented by the years since Donald Trump's first election in 2016, as nonprofits have been challenged to manage issues of inclusion, fairness, free speech, transparency, and viewpoint diversity. I will show how some organizations have gone off the rails, descending into turmoil and acrimony. But I will also show how effective leaders are navigating their way through crisis. Along the way, I hope to make the case for a brand of nonprofit leadership rooted in humility rather than hubris.

This book is divided into two sections. Part I, "A World of Pain," takes a hard look at the nonprofit sector. Here the goal is to detail some of the most common criticisms that nonprofits have engendered in recent years and acknowledge that some of these critiques have a kernel (or more) of truth to them. The nonprofit sector is far from perfect and, like any longstanding institution, it is in need of constant updating and reform. But even as we look to improve nonprofit organizations, we must be careful not to overcorrect. Criticism, taken too far, can end up undermining nonprofits instead of strengthening them.

In Part II, "A Way Through," I try to articulate what good nonprofit leadership looks like. There is of course, no single way to lead an organization. But I attempt to tease out what some of the most agile nonprofit leaders have in common. The "my way or the highway" leadership that has often been valorized in the past has run its course. Instead, nonprofit leaders must be flexible and adaptive. Central to this is an ability to bring employees along with them—leaders can no longer count on a paycheck to guarantee loyalty or performance.

While they work to exhibit greater sensitivity to the needs and demands of staff, nonprofit leaders must also strenuously resist the dangers of mission creep, ensuring that their organizations remain focused on what they do best and avoid getting ensnared in activities (and political controversies) beyond their ken. Maintaining this balance will be a key leadership challenge in the years ahead as a second Trump administration will no doubt create many issues of controversy. I close the book by offering a few ruminations inspired by Trump's first week in office in 2025.

THE STAKES ARE HIGH

I have spent my entire professional career working in the nonprofit sector. This has included helping to lead both large and small organizations, including the Center for Court Innovation and Vital City.

I am not an academic or a management consultant. I don't know much about organizational theory. For better or for worse, my perspective has been shaped by my life within the nonprofit sector. My argument is based largely on my own direct experience as well as what I have learned from observing my peers in action. Because of this background, I am, I hope, able to appreciate both the quotidian foibles and the hidden strengths of nonprofits in a way that outsiders might miss.

I talked with dozens of nonprofit executives in writing this book. In general, they are feeling much better about the sector than they were in 2020–2022, when things really seemed to be going haywire. That's good news. Still, it is worth noting that many of the people I talked with declined to be quoted by name, even when they were saying fairly anodyne things. That's not a sign of a healthy culture.

The epigraph for this book is a quotation by the singer Nick Cave about the conservative temperament. Like Cave, I am suspicious of the impulse to tear things down and generally inclined toward incremental reform rather than revolutionary change. I have written this book because I think that the American nonprofit sector is in a precarious state and that it needs conserving. In order to do that, we need to see clearly the sector's flaws and move to reform them. But we also need to protect nonprofit agencies from overcorrection and the urge to tear them down unnecessarily to begin anew.

This book was written in a spirit of pragmatic optimism. My optimism is informed by my time working within the American nonprofit sector. I have seen first-hand the good that it can do. For decades, I worked at an organization that provided alternatives to incarceration to tens of thousands of people. I have seen the impact of this work at a granular level—avoiding jail can profoundly alter the course of an individual's life, putting them on a path that facilitates education, employment, marriage, and a host of other positive outcomes. I have also seen the impact of this work on a societal level—a vibrant network of nonprofit service providers has been an important player in helping to significantly reduce incarceration (while preserving public safety) in New York over the past generation.

This is just one example of how American nonprofits are making a difference. But they can't make a difference without the active support of the public. Public trust is the sine qua non of the nonprofit sector. Without trust, nonprofits will be starved of both volunteers and donors. Without trust, they will struggle to attract the staff they need to fulfill their missions. And without trust, they won't be able to play their unique role in American society, tending to the disadvantaged, advancing knowledge and art, and prodding the country to live up to its highest ideals.

The hidden crisis facing nonprofits is the declining public confidence in the sector. If nonprofits don't reverse the trend line soon, they may be hit with a stark lesson: once trust has been lost, it is exceedingly difficult to regain. The stakes are high for nonprofit leaders. The time to act is now.

Chapter 1

Fault Lines

The TED Foundation is a nonprofit organization dedicated to spreading good ideas. It is best known for putting on "TED talks" by leading celebrity thinkers like Bill Gates and Bryan Stevenson. These speeches, which are intensively staged and produced, are so popular that they have become cliché, a shorthand way of denoting "thought leadership."

In 2023, a young writer and podcaster named Coleman Hughes received a big professional break—he was invited to give a TED talk. His speech, titled "A Case for Color Blindness," offered a straightforward argument: "We should try our best to treat people without regard to race, both in our personal lives and in our public policy."[1]

This line of thinking has a strong tradition in American civic life. As Hughes details, the philosophy of color blindness can trace its roots back to the anti-slavery movement. Perhaps the most famous articulation of this idea is Martin Luther King Jr.'s March on Washington speech, where he proclaimed, "I have a dream that my four little children will one day live in a nation where they will not be judged by the color of their skin but by the content of their character."

Many Americans are attracted to this vision. Support for a color-blind approach to policymaking is generally popular. For example, a Pew survey finds that only one in three Americans approves of selective colleges considering race in admissions decisions.[2] And ballot initiatives to advance affirmative action have tended to fare poorly, even in liberal states like California, where a 2020 referendum was soundly defeated.

But not everyone agrees with the idea that people should be treated first and foremost as individuals rather than as members of distinct racial groups. In recent years, a strong counternarrative has emerged among left-wing academics and activists who have come to see the color-blind approach as fundamentally flawed. Disappointed with the persistence of racial disparities in the United States even in the aftermath of landmark civil rights legislation, these critics argue that the only path to equality involves enacting "race conscious" policies that explicitly favor Black Americans and other marginalized groups.

Unfortunately for Hughes, a vocal group of TED employees subscribes to this view. As Hughes explains it, "The day after my talk, I heard from Chris Anderson, the head of TED. He told me that a group called 'Black@TED'—which TED's website describes as an 'Employee Resource Group that exists to provide a safe space for TED staff who identify as Black'—was 'upset' by my talk."[3] In fact, these internal critics were so miffed that they argued that TED shouldn't publish the video of Hughes's speech.

Chris Anderson, who leads TED, found himself in a dilemma. There was nothing explicitly objectionable about Hughes's talk, which fell squarely within TED's stated mission. As Anderson would later state on Twitter, "We're a nonpartisan nonprofit organization, and our mission is to offer powerful ideas to everyone in the world, not just those from within one political group. Speaking personally, as TED's ultimate decision maker, I am determined that we hold to that mission."[4]

But against that were the feelings that the talk aroused among a vocal group of TED staffers and supporters. According to Anderson,

> If someone's spent their whole life experiencing a playing field that is tilted against them, proactive policies to un-tilt that field are a ray of light. A talk arguing to dump those in favor of color-blindness can therefore seem not just wrong, but truly dangerous. So I get why some members of the TED community—and also some of our team—were upset by Coleman's talk. I see comments from people saying "That's their problem, just fire them." Give me a break. I love this team. They're smart, creative, curious and kind, and they work for TED because they believe in the importance of ideas and in TED's mission. I think it's healthy that there are sometimes heartfelt debates within the org. When those arise, the right stance is to try to work through them so that we can all learn.

What to do? Should Anderson give in to those who found the talk "dangerous" and effectively censor Hughes? Or should he go forward with publishing the speech and risk losing the support of a good chunk of his staff?

A HARD JOB BECOMES HARDER

These are the kinds of decisions that countless nonprofit executives have had to wrestle with in recent years. Running a nonprofit organization has always been difficult work. A leader must be able to articulate a vision, raise money, recruit and retain staff, manage a budget, establish an organizational culture, and many more tasks besides. None of these demands have gone away. But recent years have added new burdens to the shoulders of nonprofit leaders. The result is that a hard job has become nearly impossible.

The past decade or so has witnessed a sea change in the dynamics at many nonprofit organizations. A variety of developments have opened up new fault lines, or exacerbated existing ones, within American nonprofits:

- *Donald Trump*—The political success of Donald Trump—and the perception among many progressives that he is guilty of racism, xenophobia, and even fascism—created pressure on nonprofits to take a public stand. A failure to explicitly condemn Trump was viewed in some quarters as "complicity" with the harms wrought by his administration. In general, the Trump years have been marked by nonprofit crusading; even organizations that have traditionally thought of themselves as apolitical have been drawn into issuing political statements and engaging in social media activism.
- *#MeToo*—As with government and the private sector, #MeToo has had a major impact on the nonprofit sector, forcing many organizations to confront bad, and sometimes criminal, behavior on the part of some male supervisors.
- *Covid-19*—The pandemic required every American institution to develop new ways of doing business on the fly. Some of these accommodations were temporary, but many have proved lasting, including the expansion of remote work. In so doing, the pandemic exposed a significant gap between nonprofit staff who could easily work from home and those who could not. It also highlighted a generational divide in terms of expectations of workplace culture.

- *Black Lives Matter*—Even before the death of George Floyd, many American nonprofits were wrestling with the problem of racial disparities within the sector. Afterward, the intensity was ratcheted up even further. The result was an explosion of "anti-racist" statements and a massive investment in "diversity, equity, and inclusion" programming that transformed the language, goals, and operations of many nonprofit organizations.
- *Unionization*—Motivated by staff concerns over wages and working conditions, there has been a surge in unionization at American nonprofits in recent years. This has been part of a larger dynamic, fueled by an era of low unemployment, that has tilted the scales of labor relations in the direction of labor.
- *The War in Gaza*—The Hamas attack on Israel of October 7, 2023, and the subsequent war in Gaza, aroused strong passions within the American nonprofit sector. The response revealed a rift not just between those sympathetic to Israel and those sympathetic to the Palestinians, but between liberals concerned about antisemitism and social justice activists who do not tend to view Jews as a vulnerable minority group.

These issues have affected different organizations in different ways, but they have all tended to widen the divide between staff and management and intensify the demands on leadership.

In this book, we will look at some of the major fault lines that have roiled American nonprofits over the past decade. American nonprofits have always been affected by forces beyond their control, of course. No one gets to choose the times they live in. The nonprofit sector, which relies on government funding and private philanthropy, is particularly vulnerable to changing economic conditions, which can limit revenues and donations.

But the winds buffeting American nonprofits at the moment are different. They have had a seismic impact on the sector because they have exposed real weaknesses that have gone unaddressed for too long—many American nonprofits were, and are, in need of significant change. The critiques that union leaders, feminists, racial justice activists, and others have advanced in recent years don't come out of nowhere. There are in fact many workplaces where employees confront sexual harassment, unequal pay, racial discrimination, and other legitimate concerns. Nonprofits ignore these issues at their own peril.

Similarly, the criticisms levied by those concerned about the political drift of American nonprofits are not without merit. Except for those organizations that are explicitly conservative, American nonprofits have a tendency to attract staff who are generally left of center. The events of the last few years have conspired to exacerbate this dynamic. Many nonprofits have moved in an explicitly progressive direction. In the process, they have become inhospitable not just to Republicans, but even to many moderates and liberals who do not conform to a narrow ideological orthodoxy.

Significant reform is required within the American nonprofit sector to address these issues. Having said this, many of the complaints that have been levied against American nonprofits in recent years are exaggerated or based on isolated bad actors. Moreover, the urge for reform can be pressed too far, leading to unintended consequences that can undermine the effectiveness of nonprofits.

THREE CHALLENGES

In the pages that follow, I hope to paint a nuanced portrait of the state of the American nonprofit sector, highlighting both what needs to change and what needs to be preserved. Of all the issues that confront nonprofit leaders at the moment, there are three in particular that stand out:

Generational Change—It is difficult to talk about generations without lapsing into stereotypes. Not every Gen X-er listened to Nirvana, after all. (In fact, artists like Celine Dion and Garth Brooks sold many more records than Nirvana in the 1990s and no one outside of their immediate families thinks of them as generation-defining artists.) The Pew Research Center has recently rethought the way that it does generational research, admitting that there is no science behind the definition of generational categories.[5] A strong case can be made that generational cohorts have about as much explanatory validity as grouping people into different zodiac signs.

Still, something has shifted in the American workplace. And whether real or perceived, many managers have attributed these changes to the influence of the younger Americans who comprise the Millennial generation and Generation Z. In a widely shared interview, actress Jodie Foster captured some of the frustrations that older employers experience with young people in the workplace: "They're like, 'Nah, I'm not feeling it today, I'm gonna come in at 10.30am.' Or in emails, I'll tell them, 'This is all grammatically incorrect, did you not check your spelling?' And they're like, 'Why would I do that, isn't that kind of limiting?'"[6]

According to Jean Twenge, author of the book *Generations*, "The generation gap is larger now than it has been since the late 1960s, when the Boomers and their parents were on the other sides of a generational divide. I think that's mostly due to the fast pace of technological change."[7] It is fair to say that younger workers have brought with them a new set of expectations about how the world of work should function and how it should fit into their lives.

What kinds of working hours and conditions are acceptable? How long do you need to wait until you get to voice your opinion about the strategic direction of your agency? What should you do if the organization you work for does not reflect your values? These are the kinds of questions that young workers are posing for American organizations at the moment. In response, nonprofits are being forced to rethink how they make decisions and how they organize themselves for fear of losing talent to their competitors in a strong labor market.

Polarization—In the era of Donald Trump, talk of political polarization has dominated American editorial pages and social media platforms. Some of this has no doubt been overstated: the polling data does not support the idea that most Americans have become diehard leftists or reactionary conservatives. Indeed, vast numbers of Americans remain politically disengaged and more Americans identify as moderates and independents than as either Democrats or Republicans.

Nonetheless, there are clear signs that educational polarization has developed into a major factor in American life, with college-educated Americans becoming solidly Democratic and the non-college-educated being drawn increasingly into the Republican camp.

The number of Americans with a bachelor's degree has increased dramatically in our lifetimes—in 1960, only 7.7% of Americans were college graduates; today that number stands at 37.7%.[8] Those with college degrees may still comprise a minority of the American population but they dominate the institutions that hold cultural and political power in the United States. This includes influential nonprofit organizations.

In *Polarized by Degrees*, political scientists Matt Grossman and David A. Hopkins argue that the principal dividing line in American life these days is not race, geography, or income but rather education; they believe that the diploma divide is one of the main drivers of American polarization. They write:

> Many high-status institutions—including . . . nonprofit institutions—have become overwhelmingly populated by well-educated professionals just as those actors have become politically distinct and more identified with advancing cultural liberalism. Unsurprisingly, conservatives no longer see these institutions as open to their political ideas, but instead as powerful opponents in the culture war.[9]

The federal tax code prohibits nonprofits from supporting candidates for political office, which means that most organizations are technically being accurate when they say that they are "non-partisan." But this doesn't mean that nonprofits are neutral institutions. Indeed, it is often easy to discern the political orientation of nonprofits from a glance at their websites or their social media feeds.

As many nonprofits move to the left, it becomes harder and harder for them to attract staffers who are conservatives. Even some liberals have begun to feel unwelcome in the sector. This presents a number of challenges. First, it inhibits good decision-making, as ideas are not subject to scrutiny and challenge from a range of perspectives. Just as important, it means that nonprofits run the risk of becoming detached from popular opinion, further feeding public distrust in the sector.

Race—"Nonprofits are ruled by white people," declared the *Stanford Social Innovation Review* in 2011.[10] Things have changed quite a bit since then, but the basic point still holds: the leadership of many nonprofits, both at the staff and the board level, tends to be dominated by white people.

The emergence of Black Lives Matter has focused increased attention on this uncomfortable truth. In response, nonprofit organizations across the country have made massive investments in diversity, equity, and inclusion (DEI) initiatives. HR departments were transformed into "people and culture" departments and tasked with remaking institutional cultures. Consultants were hired to perform top-to-bottom organizational reviews to identify any disparities in programming, hiring, or salaries. Mandatory training sessions were convened to teach staff about implicit bias, microaggressions, and a host of other race-related topics.

Changes of this scale almost always engender backlash. DEI has been no exception to this rule. At first, the criticisms could mostly be dismissed as the resistance of conservatives who would oppose any effort to improve fairness or celebrate the changing demographics of the United States. But as the emotions of 2020 began to fade, more-informed critiques began to emerge, suggesting that there was little evidence to support the efficacy of diversity trainings and that DEI initiatives were helping to undermine social cohesion. By 2022, the *Harvard Business Review* was announcing "The Failure of the DEI-Industrial Complex."[11]

All of this makes for tricky terrain for the typical nonprofit executive. It is no longer tenable to ignore or minimize the role that race plays in internal operations, as many nonprofits were able to do in the years prior to the emergence of Black Lives

Matter. High-functioning nonprofits should be trying to ensure that they are attracting talented staffers of all backgrounds and that diverse perspectives are voiced when key organizational decisions are made. But recent years have also seen a number of organizations go off the rails, spending inordinate time and resources wrestling with how race plays out internally—energy and money that would be better spent trying to accomplish their missions.

NO-WIN SCENARIOS

The three principal challenges that nonprofit leaders face now—race, generational change, and polarization—are overlapping. Younger staffers are more likely to be people of color and more likely to seek race-conscious policymaking from their organizations. Those concerned about the leftward drift of nonprofits tend to be white and older. And so on.

The controversy over Coleman Hughes's TED talk exemplifies this reality. Each of the three challenges was at work. Hughes's speech was explicitly focused on the question of how to achieve racial justice. Hughes was advocating for an idea—a color blind approach to policy—that polling suggests most Americans endorse. Younger staffers at TED, many of them people of color, viewed the issue differently than both the general public and the Boomer chief executive of TED, Chris Anderson, who was born in 1957.

Hovering over the whole conflict was the question of accountability—Who gets to decide what TED publishes? The leader of TED? The staff of the organization? The vox populi as expressed on social media? (These kinds of questions will come up again in the Conclusion as we wrestle with the challenge of accountability in nonprofits.)

As Anderson tried to work his way through this minefield, he was eager to fashion a compromise. He ended up asking Hughes to participate in a supplemental debate with *New York Times* reporter Jamelle Bouie, which Hughes agreed to do, with some hesitation. As Hughes later recounted,

> [Anderson] conceded that his employees' anger stemmed from political bias, but nevertheless asked me to agree to an atypical release strategy: TED would release the debate and the talk as separate videos, but at the same time. He sold this idea to me as a way to amplify my talk—as if this atypical release strategy were conceived for my benefit. That made little sense to me. The reality, I told him, was that these nonstandard release strategies were intended not to amplify my message but to dilute it. After all, the whole genesis of this debacle was the fact that certain TED staffers wanted to nix my talk altogether—and Anderson feared an internal firestorm if my talk were released normally. Clearly, the release proposals being pressed upon me were conceived in order to placate angry staffers, not in order to amplify my message.[12]

But then, when Hughes's TED talk was ultimately released, it received a suspiciously small number of views relative to other TED talks. When this happened, Hughes deduced that TED was not actively promoting his speech the way it did other talks. So he decided to go public with his side of the story. The result was a week or two of controversy that featured many of the hallmarks of contemporary internet kerfuffles, including angry podcasts, tweet storms, and competing essays in *The Free Press*.

For many observers, Anderson was cast as the villain of the piece, a craven leader too weak to stand up to the woke mob in his organization. Jesse Singal, a popular writer and podcaster, expressed this sentiment in his essay, "Organizational Leaders like Chris Anderson Should Stop Indulging Their Most Hysterical Employees." His conclusion: "Chris Anderson botched it every single step of the way."[13]

But is this true? If Anderson intentionally failed to promote Hughes's talk, then he did indeed make a mistake. But Anderson has disputed this characterization, and no one outside of TED has the facts to determine whether he is lying or telling the truth.

Otherwise, Anderson made a set of reasonable choices designed to protect the integrity of his organization and maintain staff morale. Most importantly, he did not yield to demands to censor Hughes's speech. This would have been a clear violation of the principles of non-partisanship and knowledge dissemination that are central to TED's mission.

At the same time, Anderson demonstrated to staff that he had listened to their concerns and that their voices mattered within his institution. The compromise he forged probably pleased no one. But from where I sit, it achieved what he needed it to achieve.

Anderson endured several days of people shouting at him online. But the controversy soon died down and Anderson went back to work. TED may have taken a small reputational hit, but it too has moved on to bigger and better things.

The Coleman Hughes imbroglio had some attributes that were unique to TED, but the truth is that in recent years many nonprofit leaders have had to confront dilemmas similar to Anderson's, where competing values and important stakeholders with conflicting views have combined to create what are essentially no-win situations.

Anderson's approach satisfied neither the social justice warriors on his staff nor the anti-woke scolds on Twitter. But it did succeed in navigating TED through choppy waters without either abandoning the organization's core values or sparking a widespread staff revolt. For this, he deserves praise, not vilification.

We will return to this lesson—that a moderate, thoughtful brand of management that resists capitulation to both internal and external critics is the best way to deal with the myriad challenges that nonprofit leaders face today—again as this book proceeds.

Chapter 2

The Generational Divide

One of the things that I did almost every year after I became the executive director of the Center for Court Innovation in 2002 was to meet with participants in a fellowship program run by the Coro Leadership Center. I felt a special connection to the program, which offers leadership training to early-career professionals, because I had been a participant myself when I was in my twenties.

Each year, a dozen Coro Fellows would visit me in my office for an hour or so, asking me questions about the work of the Center for Court Innovation. While these were all young people with an interest in public service, very few of them knew anything about criminal justice. That made sense—criminal justice was a pretty niche issue in the early 2000s.

By the time 2015 rolled around, however, things had changed. The New Jim Crow *was a national bestseller. Black Lives Matter had successfully focused national attention on racism and police violence. When I met with the Coro Fellows that year, I sensed a different kind of energy in the room—I was no longer talking to a group of people who had no opinion about criminal justice.*

When the group asked me to outline the problems that the Center for Court Innovation was trying to address, I talked about a justice system that processed cases like widgets in a factory and that too often defaulted to incarceration when other, better options were possible. Out of the corner of my eye, I saw a hand shoot up. I paused to enable the young woman, a recent graduate of an elite liberal arts college, to speak. "There's only one thing wrong with the criminal justice system," she declared with an air of finality, "And that's structural racism." That basically ended the conversation.

This kind of assertion has become commonplace in the nonprofit sector in recent years. The problem is not that this young woman is wrong—reasonable people can disagree about whether racism is the only, or even the primary, thing wrong with the justice system. The problem is the attitude of incuriosity and the implicit insistence that there is only one correct answer to a given question. As progressive Millennial and Gen Z employees have come to dominate more and more organizations, the short-circuiting of debate and defaulting to left-wing ideology has become a real hazard for the nonprofit sector.

***

Woody Allen famously joked that 80% of success in life is just showing up. As anyone who goes to work every day can attest, the challenge is that just showing up is much harder than it looks. Commuting can be time-consuming and expensive. Your co-workers are often boring or incompetent. Invariably you are asked to perform tasks that seem useless or stultifying or stressful. Your superiors may not recognize or appreciate your value. The list goes on.

None of the pressures of the working life go away just because you happen to work at a nonprofit. Indeed, nonprofit employment often adds challenges to the pile. Working for a mission-driven organization usually means making less money than you would in the private or public sector, which can create financial hardship and induce resentment.

And then there is the problem of expectations.

Almost every nonprofit talks a good game about their values and the world that they are trying to create—a world typically defined by justice, transparency, and democracy. And then you go to work at a nonprofit and you discover that life is unfair, that many decisions are made behind closed doors, and that no one is going to ask you for your opinion about a whole bunch of important stuff.

The sad truth is that there is a long history of autocratic and even abusive behavior among nonprofit leaders. The case of Morris Dees, the co-founder and longtime leader of the Southern Poverty Law Center, is instructive.

A BUFFET OF INJUSTICES

Based in Montgomery, Alabama, the Southern Poverty Law Center is one of the most prominent nonprofit organizations in the country. Their mission is to combat racism by tracking right-wing extremism and engaging in impact litigation designed to protect civil rights.[1]

Dees, one of the organization's co-founders, led the organization for nearly 50 years. (Reigns of this length are often a warning sign that leadership has grown too entrenched and powerful. This is a subject we will return to in Chapter 9.) Dees made any number of wise strategic decisions over the years, including winning a series of legal fights that damaged the finances of the Ku Klux Klan and enhanced the Law Center's visibility.

But Dees's true gift was as a fundraiser. Dees got his start in direct marketing. In fact, he was so successful that he had already made a small fortune before starting the Southern Poverty Law Center in 1971. (Dees was ultimately elected to the Direct Marketing Hall of Fame.) Dees knew that a Southern organization fighting the Klan and other extremist groups was a cause that would be appealing to a broad audience of Northern liberals, and he worked hard to figure out how best to reach them.

The level of thought and sophistication that went into a typical Southern Poverty Law Center fundraising appeal could be impressive. A former employee reported that the organization used several low-value stamps when it was mailing out its appeals in an effort to convey that it could barely afford to cobble together 35 cents worth of postage.[2] Another former employee claimed that Dees, born into a Baptist family, would use his Jewish-sounding middle name (Seligman) prominently when mailing to zip codes with large Jewish populations. "We just run our business like a business," said Dees in an interview with *The Progressive*. "Whether you're selling cakes or causes, it's all the same."[3]

A 2017 article in *Politico* described Dees this way:

> Smooth, publicity-savvy and detail-averse, Dees is a marketing genius whose greatest success may be selling his own persona as a crusader—a skill on display across the street from the SPLC's office, where a black granite memorial to the casualties of the civil rights movement proclaims it was built by the Morris Dees Legacy Fund. Inside the memorial's gift shop, visitors will find on the wall a framed photo of Dees staring off into the distance, looking equal parts pensive and saintly. On a shelf next to SPLC-branded water bottles and mugs, the same image of Dees reappears in another frame; it's also printed on nearby postcards, which are available for purchase. Touches such as these have led some journalists to nickname Dees, with irony, "the Mother Teresa of Montgomery."[4]

The Law Center's success as a fundraising shop is legendary. They have hundreds of thousands of donors and rake in tens of millions of dollars each year. The organization's endowment now exceeds $730 million.

All of that money gave Dees a lot of leeway. This is a cold truth about the nonprofit sector: in an industry that relies on donations, those that bring in the money have the most value. Successful fundraising covers up for a lot of sins. Or at least it did, up until relatively recently.

In 2019, Dees was fired. In a statement, the Southern Poverty Law Center said that the organization was "committed to ensuring that the conduct of our staff reflects the mission of the organization and the values we hope to instill in the world. When one of our own fails to meet those standards, no matter his or her role in the organization, we take it seriously and must take appropriate action."[5]

Writing in *The New Yorker*, former Law Center employee Bob Moser painted a dismal portrait of life at the organization. According to Moser, the leadership of the agency was almost uniformly white and the support staff almost exclusively Black. Dees regularly propositioned young female employees. Among a slew of anonymous quotes in the piece, one former Law Center employee, speculating on the reason for Dees's dismissal, said, "It could be racial, sexual, financial—that place was a virtual buffet of injustices."[6] The *Los Angeles Times* reported that dozens of employees had complained about "allegations of mistreatment, sexual harassment, gender discrimination, and racism" at the organization.[7]

The Southern Poverty Law Center is not a typical nonprofit. Very few organizations have such a high profile and such a large endowment. And most nonprofit leaders have not been accused of the kind of sustained misbehavior that has been alleged at the Law Center.

Still, what happened at the Law Center is an extreme version of something that has gripped a large number of nonprofit organizations in recent years: younger employees actively revolting against leadership that they view as racist, sexist, autocratic, and out-of-touch.

The rebellion is not unfounded. The nonprofit sector is vulnerable to three critiques in particular:

- *Sexual Harassment*: While the nonprofit workforce tends to skew female, that doesn't mean that women are treated uniformly well within the sector. For example, one in four female nonprofit fundraisers say that they have experienced sexual harassment.[8] The Humane Society, Habitat for Humanity, the United Way, and the Red Cross are just a few examples of leading nonprofit organizations that have parted ways with executives accused of sexual harassment or abuse in recent years. There is a reason why the #MeToo movement came for the nonprofit sector.
- *Racial Disparities*: The nonprofit sector is also not immune to the problem of racial disparities. It is hard to come by good data on the racial composition of nonprofit executive teams, but the preponderance of evidence suggests that, while the sector has made significant strides in recent years, organizational leadership continues to be largely white. The Building Movement Project, an activist organization, argues that the percentage of nonprofit CEOs who are people of color stands at roughly 20%. They also suggest that one in two people of color think their careers have been negatively affected by their race or ethnicity.[9] I will take up the question of race and nonprofits at greater length in Chapter 4.

- *Wage Inequality*: Given the diversity of the sector, it is also difficult to find good data comparing nonprofit salaries to salaries in the private and public sectors. But there is some evidence to suggest that, at the bottom of the wage scale, many nonprofit workers are not earning enough to afford a decent living. This problem is particularly acute in places, like New York City, with a high cost of living. The Human Services Council, an association of New York nonprofits, argues that one in five nonprofit human service workers receives SNAP benefits (aka "food stamps"). They also argue that nonprofit human service staff earn about 71% of what their peers in government make.[10]

It is of course appropriate that nonprofit leaders who engage in discrimination and abuse and don't pay their staff adequately come under scrutiny. If the allegations are true, the Morris Dees of the world deserve to be defenestrated.

But let's imagine for a second that you run an organization that has a good proportion of Black senior staff, no record of sexual harassment, and a history of paying people decently. Does that mean that your younger employees have been happy campers over the last decade? The answer is no.

Staff unrest has come for good and bad leaders alike. When you talk to the executives of nonprofit agencies about their young workers these days, the dominant theme is exhaustion and exasperation. No one has gotten a free pass. According to William Galston, a senior fellow at the Brookings Institution:

> I've had the chance to talk to several presidents and executive directors of established left-leaning centers and groups.

> They all tell versions of the same story: Around 2015, something changed. The young people they were hiring were focused on issues of race, gender, and identity as never before, and they were impatient with—even scornful of—what they regarded as the timid incrementalism of the organizations' leaders. They wanted equity (as they defined it) immediately. They were acutely sensitive to what they saw as microaggressions, including the use of terms to identify different groups that they regarded as out of date and insulting. They were prickly, quick to take offense and to see malign motives rather than inadvertent mistakes. This generation gap has forced leaders to devote unprecedented time and energy to internal governance, sometimes to the detriment of their organization's mission.[11]

Generation after generation of workers have had to grapple with the realities of life in the nonprofit sector, but this is the first generation to actively rise up in concerted protest. Why is that? What's different about the young people currently in their twenties and thirties?

BY THE NUMBERS

A surge of births in the aftermath of World War II created what has become known as the Baby Boom generation. As they have aged, this generation has had an outsized impact in the United States. For example, they are often credited with helping to create the contemporary idea of the teenage years as a separate space between childhood and adulthood that could be the subject of targeted consumer marketing. The Baby Boomers are also the generation that is largely responsible for the turbulent 1960s, when many of them were in their college years and the civil rights movement and Vietnam War protests were at their peak.

Some of the Baby Boomers forged by the passion and activism of the 1960s ended up in the nonprofit sector. They have been a dominant force in the sector ever since. According to Glassdoor, Baby Boomers outnumbered every other generation in the workforce from the late 1970s until late 2011. The oldest Boomers reached retirement age around that time. As Boomers started to retire, there was a brief window, 2012–2018, when there were more Generation Xers in the workforce than there were workers from any other generation. But Millennials overtook them at that point and are now poised to dominate the workforce for many years to come.[12]

The Millennial generation is typically defined as those born between 1981 and 1996. The sheer size of this generation (Pew estimates that there are more than 72 million Millennials) almost guarantees that they will have a larger impact than the smaller Generation X that preceded them.

The Millennial generation is distinguished from their predecessors in several important ways. In general, they are better educated—around 4 in 10 Millennials have a college degree, compared to only 25% of Baby Boomers when they were the same age. They are slower to own their own houses than prior generations and are starting families later too. Indeed, Pew estimates that if current patterns continue, one in four Millennials will have never married by the time they reach their 40s—a record high. Millennials are also more racially and ethnically diverse than prior generations. The share of non-Hispanic white Millennials is just

55%—down from 64% in the Silent Generation—a shift driven by interracial marriage and increased immigration among Hispanic and Asian populations. All of these trends will continue as Generation Z increasingly comes into the workforce—they are set to be the most diverse and most well-educated generation yet.[13]

But it isn't just their sheer numbers that give Millennial and younger workers power in the workplace. They have also benefited from an exceptionally strong labor market in the United States. While the job market has experienced two seismic shocks over the past two decades—the recession sparked by the 2008 financial crisis and the Covid-19 pandemic—there has been robust job growth in recent years. In 2023, the Commerce Department announced that the unemployment rate was lower than it had been in more than a half century.[14]

With available workers in short supply, the balance of power in the workplace has tipped in the direction of labor. According to labor economist Aaron Sojourner, "Workers quitting their jobs is a signal that they feel like they have a lot of options." He estimates that in 2022, the ratio of workers quitting compared to workers being laid off reached an all-time high, with 3.3 workers quitting for every worker that was fired.[15] Put simply, Millennial employees have the ability to say to their employers, "take this job and shove it" in a way that older workers never did.

BORN DIGITAL

One of the things that distinguishes Millennials from preceding generations is that they are the first to have spent their formative years online. No one in their thirties in the United States remembers a time without computers, smartphones, and the

Internet. Young people today navigate the online world intuitively because they have grown up within it.

This has had all sorts of salutary effects for nonprofit organizations, which increasingly rely on Millennials and Generation Z-ers to construct databases, create apps, manage social media feeds, and much more. It is safe to say that the digital expertise of young people is now essential to the effective operation of the nonprofit sector.

But young workers' digital savvy also presents challenges. Millennials have grown up with the ability to shape their online environment to their needs. They have gotten used to tailoring their iPhones, their social media feeds, and their Netflix cues to meet their distinct aesthetics. It is only natural for them to assume that they should also be able to make their workplaces reflect their idiosyncratic values and preferences. For older managers, this may read as entitlement. For the Millennials, this is just logic at work.

One leader of an educational nonprofit told me, "Young people have grown up in a virtual world. If you are sitting at home, interacting with people through a computer, the organization that you work for is an abstraction. It's just faces on a screen. It is almost impossible to build culture or loyalty in that context."

Indeed, many organizations have struggled to get Millennial and Gen Z employees even to come in to the office. A 2021 survey found that fully 90% of workers born after 1981 did not want to return to full-time office work following the Covid-19 pandemic.[16]

The combination of the pandemic and exposure to social media may present unique challenges to the mental well-being of the young people who increasingly staff our nonprofit organizations. A 2019 survey found that almost all (95%) Millennials use social media, and the vast majority (86%) do so on a daily basis.[17] Many worry that this level of social media use is bad for users. In May of 2023, Surgeon General Vivek H. Murthy issued a public warning that social media poses a risk to mental well-being. And there is some research that suggests that the mental health of those born in the 1990s is worse than the generations that preceded them—and not getting better as they age.[18]

All of these forces combine to create real challenges for nonprofit agencies. To attract, retain, and get the best out of their Millennial and Gen Z workers, they have had to change their expectations about showing up for work, alter the ways they communicate, and invest in additional mental health resources. Perhaps every generation ends up reshaping the world of work, but the Millennial generation has done so particularly quickly and profoundly.

GENERATION ANGST

There is an old piece of folk wisdom that goes something like this: If you are not a liberal when you are 20, then you have no heart. But if you are still a liberal at 40, you have no brain. The evidence suggests that young people today have plenty of heart. Although the Republicans did better with younger voters in 2024 than many expected, Millennials and Gen Z-ers are more likely than older generations to disapprove of Donald Trump, to believe that government should do more to solve people's problems, and to think that increasing diversity is good for society.[19]

This should come as little surprise; after all, there is a long tradition of young people being more left-wing than their elders. But something feels different about the political orientation of this generation. Perhaps they hold their convictions more fiercely than their predecessors. Or perhaps they have just lost faith in American institutions. Their experience, at a formative moment in their development, of the financial collapse of 2008, and the subsequent struggle of the American government to restore the economy and punish those who were responsible, may have set the tone for what has followed.

According to a survey by Ernst & Young and the Economic Innovation Group, Millennials express low levels of confidence in nearly every American institution—for example, only 27% of Millennials express "a lot of confidence" in the justice system. Rabbi David Wolpe, a visiting scholar at Harvard Divinity School, thinks that greater transparency, fueled by 24-hour news coverage and social media, has revealed that the leaders of many crucial American institutions are flawed at best, and fundamentally corrupt at worse. "When we tell kids a story, they don't believe us," says Wolpe. "Why should they? They have grown up in a world where all the stories turned out not to be true."[20]

In addition to low levels of trust in institutions, Millennials also express high rates of anxiety about the future and about the economy. This, along with a surge of mental health issues, has led researchers to label Millennials "Generation Angst."[21]

Young people bring both their psychological issues and their political commitments with them to work. Unlike previous generations, they are also bringing the expectation that their workplaces will align with their values. When they do not . . . that's when the trouble starts.

Sometimes the trouble is modest—a Deloitte survey reveals that nearly 40% of Millennial and Gen Z staffers say that they have rejected work assignments due to ethical concerns.[22] But sometimes the trouble is truly disruptive. Technology has played a facilitating role, allowing internal discontent to coalesce (via Slack, for example) and be broadcast to the world (via social media). As *Atlantic* staff writer Thomas Chatterton Williams has noted, "One of the less remarked upon features of recent years throughout institutional culture—corporations, NGOs, universities, museums, publications—is that basically no one is willing to accept simply being a junior member of the hierarchy anymore. The proverbial intern arrives at training now with a list of demands that will align the institution with her values."[23]

In a viral 2022 essay in *The Intercept*, writer Ryan Grim claimed that "It's hard to find a Washington-based progressive organization that hasn't been in tumult or isn't currently in tumult."[24] The tumult has included internal advocacy campaigns to change organizational cultures, to fire executives, and to launch unions—even within small, white-collar nonprofits. "So much energy has been devoted to the internal strife and internal bullshit that it's had a real impact on the ability for groups to deliver," one nonprofit leader told *The Intercept*.

For many nonprofit executives, this activist energy, focused as it is on internal targets rather than addressing social problems in the outside world, seems misplaced. According to Margaret Egan, the executive director of the Women's Prison Association,

> I would characterize the generational gap as a difference in expectations. Junior staff seem to have an expectation that the organization's top priority is serving the staff, while leadership is expecting the staff's top priority to be serving the participants. I'm sure there is an element of "kids these days" at play here, but something has changed over the last 15–20 years. It is certainly critical to provide staff with the appropriate support needed to effectively serve the participants. And yet, there are practical realities to how much support organizations can provide,

> particularly as government continues to not fully fund contracted services. When those expectations and reality collide, there seems to be a knee-jerk perception of malevolence on the part of leadership, rather than an understanding of the delicate balance that leadership is often trying to strike.

Off the record, nonprofit executives complain that junior staffers fail to recognize that most nonprofits are fragile institutions that cannot take their audiences, their funders, or indeed their very existence for granted. Writing about rising populism, *Financial Times* columnist Janan Ganesh managed to capture the spirit of the critique that many executives have of the young staffers currently disrupting nonprofit life: "None of these people actively desires civilizational meltdown. They just under-rate the prospect of it happening as an inadvertent result of their actions. How could they not? Unintended consequences, the precariousness of order, the independent momentum of ideas: to keep these dangers in mind takes a bitterer experience of history than is available to most people under 90. . . . The generational loss of caution is a mass phenomenon, not just an elite one."[25] Young nonprofit staffers don't realize that, in many cases, they are the metaphorical bull in the china shop—more powerful than they know, operating in an environment that is more delicate than they imagine.

Good intentions and progressive values offer no inoculation from the spirit of disruption that Millennials and Gen Z-ers have brought to the nonprofit workplace. A case in point is Youth on Boards, Action on Climate (YOB).

Launched in 2022 by a small intergenerational team, YOB was an effort to place young people on the boards of nonprofits and companies in Maine. The motivating idea was that bringing younger voices into the room would help shift organizational thinking around climate decisions, since young people have to worry about long-term future impacts in a way that older people do not. There were good reasons to think that YOB would succeed: it had a straightforward agenda and its goals seemed eminently achievable. But after less than two years, the effort fell apart.

The primary culprit was not so much politics—basically everyone involved thought of themselves as progressive—but a dispute about whether social justice should be prioritized always and everywhere. YOB was co-led by a Gen Z-er and a Baby Boomer who ended up disagreeing on this question. Writing a post-mortem for the *Stanford Social Innovation Review*, Steve Kaagan (the Baby Boomer co-leader) and John Hagan (another Boomer who ran the nonprofit that housed YOB) argued that their twenty-something colleagues were guilty of "overreach" when they sought to expand the mission of YOB to include addressing "harmful systems of power, systems of oppression, and ageist paternalistic power structures." According to Kaagan and Hagan:

> Our opposition to expanding YOB's purpose to take on harmful systems of power was regarded by other members of the team as causing harm. This notion of harm, resulting from what we considered a legitimate disagreement, was new to us. . . . We would never intentionally harm anyone, especially colleagues with whom we had worked well and respected. But in today's world there is a nebulous line between "debating ideas" and "causing harm." As our internal disagreement over ideology proliferated we unwittingly found ourselves on the wrong side of the line.[26]

Is it possible for nonprofit organizations to avoid intergenerational conflict? Probably not. Internal disagreement driven by the passions of Millennials and Generation Z will probably be a fact of nonprofit life for some years to come. But intergenerational conflict does not have to be debilitating, as the chapters ahead will show.

Chapter 3

Polarization

In November 2013, Bill de Blasio was elected mayor of New York City. Policing was a central issue in the campaign—under the previous mayor, Michael Bloomberg, the NYPD had dramatically expanded the use of "stop and frisk," a policy shift that was decried as racist by many critics and ultimately deemed unconstitutional by a federal judge.

Coming into office, one of the top priorities for de Blasio's new police commissioner, Bill Bratton, was to repair the damage that had been done to community relations by the overuse of stop and frisk. As part of this effort, Bratton selected Susan Herman to serve as the NYPD's first-ever "deputy commissioner of collaborative policing." Herman was an unusual choice: she had no experience patrolling the streets as a police officer. But what she did have was decades of experience with community development and victim services, much of it in the nonprofit sector.

I had crossed paths with Susan a number of times over the years. We weren't close buddies, but I knew Susan well enough that when her appointment was announced I reached out to her to see if she would speak at a staff meeting at the Center for Court Innovation. I was a little surprised when she immediately accepted even though she was in her first days in office.

Susan was great at the staff meeting. She talked about her desire to "drain the moat" that metaphorically separated the NYPD's headquarters from the rest of the world. She articulated a commitment to restoring public trust and engaging with nonprofits and community groups in new ways. And she graciously answered questions from the floor.

Reflecting afterward, it seemed to me that it had been a good day for my organization. A high-ranking police official had chosen to go out of her way to spend time at the Center for Court Innovation, which spoke to our growing influence in New York City. And the vision she expressed was wholly consistent with the Center's values. What could be better?

Unfortunately, some staff members at the Center did not share my perspective. Why had I "platformed" an NYPD official, they wondered. Why was the Center partnering with a racist institution? Didn't that make us complicit?

The feedback caught me by surprise. I don't want to over-egg the batter—only a few people complained—but it was one of my first indications that there was a contingent within the organization that saw the world very differently than I did. As the years went on, this contingent would grow in size and influence. By the time I left the Center in 2020, I don't think I would have felt comfortable inviting a police official to a staff meeting—the reception they would have received would have been too hostile.

This dynamic is not unique to the Center for Court Innovation. In recent years, staff members at many nonprofit organizations have become more vocal about advancing a progressive political agenda. And many nonprofit executives have responded the way that I did: by subtly changing their behavior to accommodate this emergent sensibility. The end result is a more orthodox nonprofit sector, where a much narrower band of ideas can be verbalized and debated.

***

You may be asking: Who cares? Why is this a problem?

In truth, the political atmosphere within any given nonprofit is of little concern to the rest of the world. But when the same thing happens over and over again, across a variety of nonprofits in different settings, the cumulative impact can be significant. As nonprofits become increasingly hostile environments for conservatives, moderates, and the disengaged, the ripple effects are felt both internally and externally. The result is that nonprofits are both victims and purveyors of polarization.

YES-MEN, GROUPTHINK, AND ECHO CHAMBERS

There has been a big push to diversify the leadership of nonprofits in recent years. Much of this push has been framed as an effort to improve organizational decision-making. The logic is compelling: An all-male hospital leadership group may struggle to understand the nuances of female reproductive health issues. An all-white team at a polling firm may not intuitively understand the way that some Black Americans feel about the police. Etcetera.

The same rationale applies to ideology: decision-making groups comprised exclusively of conservatives or progressives would benefit from hearing the perspectives of those who don't share their underlying assumptions. The need for diversity of thought is particularly acute because research suggests that as groups become more ideologically homogeneous, they also tend to become more extreme. This is the problem of belief polarization.

Robert Talisse, the author of *Overdoing Democracy: Why We Must Put Politics in Its Place,* describes the problem this way:

> Belief polarization is the cognitive phenomenon by which interactions with like-minded people transform us into more extreme versions of ourselves. To put it another way, when we talk only to others who share our views, we each come to hold more extreme versions of those views. Yes-men, groupthink and echo chambers can radicalize us.[1]

Humans are social animals. We are hard-wired to seek out people who think like we do. But while this instinct might make sense for us as individuals, there are real dangers when organizations engage in this same behavior. At a certain point, as an organization becomes less ideologically diverse, everyone who is a part of the organization feels enormous pressure to conform to the dominant viewpoint within the agency. Dissenters hold their tongues, even if they have valid critiques or suggestions to offer. And those who already subscribe to the dominant viewpoint become more and more confident and extreme in their beliefs.

The urge to signal loyalty to whatever group we are a part of is an understandable one. Viewed positively, it can help bind organizations together and move them forward. But there is a flip side. The urge to conformity can also undermine the health of an organization and create a mob mentality. This kind of pernicious effect is often invisible to those inside the bubble. According to Talisse, "When we surround ourselves with people who are more or less just like us politically, we become more fervent advocates of our political view . . . it's almost like a magic trick in a way because people often don't feel it happening to them. They don't recognize that they walked into the room to have a conversation with like-minded people thinking one thing, and they emerged thinking a slightly more extreme version of that thing. . . . When you're in the grip of it, you don't recognize it. That's how it does its job."[2]

What does it look like when an organization is in the grips of belief polarization? Bronx Defenders offers a case study.

A RACIST, A COLONIZER, AND A KAREN

Bronx Defenders is an organization that was born of disruption. Founded in 1997, Bronx Defenders was built on a critique of traditional public defense practice. As an alternative, they helped to pioneer "holistic defense"—the idea that in order to effectively serve low-income clients, defense attorneys have to be able to represent them in a range of court proceedings (not just criminal, but housing and family court as well) and offer supportive social services in a welcoming community environment.

But Bronx Defenders is the product of another kind of disruption as well. The name Rudy Giuliani does not figure prominently in the organization's literature about itself, but, ironically, Bronx Defenders owes a great debt to the now-notorious politician.

When he was the mayor of New York City, Giuliani decided to change the way that the City provided public defense services. Angered by a defense attorney strike in 1994, Giuliani sought to punish the Legal Aid Society, the nonprofit organization that effectively served as the public defenders of New York City. Instead of a single, citywide contract—a process that inherently favored the incumbent holder of the contract—the Giuliani administration issued a "request for proposals" for borough-based defense providers. This RFP introduced greater competition into the marketplace and helped create space (and funding) for Bronx Defenders and other smaller defense organizations to exist. In the years since then, Bronx Defenders has thrived, developing a reputation for both innovation and fierce adversarialism.

While they are a well-established part of the criminal justice landscape, Bronx Defenders rarely intruded into the larger public consciousness in New York City. That started to change in 2021.

In May of that year, Shannon Cumberbatch, an executive who worked on diversity and equity issues at the organization, sent around an email "in solidarity" with "our comrades" in Palestine. According to Cumberbatch, "The present reality of the displacement, disenfranchisement and military violence happening abroad is reminiscent of the settler colonialism, state violence and sanctioned genocide weaponized against Native and people of color in the United States."

Cumberbatch's email offended Debbie Jonas, a Jewish lawyer at Bronx Defenders with two children who had served in the Israel Defense Forces. She asked Justine Olderman, the executive director of Bronx Defenders, to issue some sort of corrective. When Olderman demurred, Jonas leaked Cumberbatch's email to a local politician, who started to raise questions about why tax dollars were being used to support the organization. In response, Olderman issued a statement supporting Cumberbatch, saying that "our naming and amplifying the suffering of Palestinian people in an email to staff . . . should be understood as an intentional effort to center the experiences of BIPOC and other marginalized people . . . [and] an intentional effort to raise awareness about the way that the issues we work on at The Bronx Defenders are connected to larger events and movements in the country and across the globe.[3]

Two years later, Bronx Defenders was back in the news. In March 2023, it was revealed that Debbie Jonas had sued Bronx Defenders for discrimination, alleging that she had been called "a racist, a colonizer, and a Karen" by staff at Bronx Defenders after they discovered that she was the source of the media leak. "I was cursed and badgered until I could no longer stand the hostility," said Jonas, who had worked at Bronx Defenders for eight years.[4] Bronx Defenders settled the case for $170,000, issued an apology, and agreed to provide training in antisemitism for its staff.

If Justine Olderman hoped that this would be the end of the ordeal, she was dead wrong. The mandatory antisemitism training she had agreed to as part of the settlement was a disaster. According to the *New York Times*, resentful participants broke out into a chant of "From the river to the sea, Palestine will be free" during the session.[5]

The issue wouldn't go away. Shortly after the October 7th Hamas attack on Israel, the union representing Bronx Defenders staffers issued a statement accusing Israel of ethnic cleansing. "We refuse to decontextualize these atrocities committed by Israel and we condemn any attempts to create false equivalencies between the oppressed and the oppressor," the statement read.[6]

Given the feverish political environment in the fall of 2023, the union statement was a bit like chumming the water—a feeding frenzy ensued. The *New York Post* editorial board asked: "Why is a public defenders union siding with terrorists?" A pro-Israel group circulated a petition demanding the defunding of Bronx Defenders. In civil court, some lawyers refused to negotiate with attorneys from Bronx Defenders.

Bronx Defenders, recognizing the danger to the institution, sent a cease-and-desist letter to the union and issued a statement distancing the organization from the union's position. But the drama is still ongoing—in 2024, Congresswoman Virginia Foxx, chair of the House Committee on Education and the Workforce, announced she would look into the union's actions to determine whether the union was properly representing the views of all of its members.

The point here is not to adjudicate the war in Gaza. Reasonable people can reach different conclusions about the conflict. But there is little question that the entire saga has damaged Bronx Defenders' reputation and threatened both its funding and effectiveness. It will be some time before the organization is able to move past the controversy.

How did this happen? Why was Bronx Defenders torn apart by a political issue that has limited, if any, connection to the core work of the organization, which, after all, is to provide legal assistance to people in the Bronx?

The internal dynamics of any organization are opaque to outside observers. No doubt, the meltdown at Bronx Defenders was the byproduct of a negative alchemy produced by specific circumstances and personalities unique to the organization.

Still, even as an outsider, it is easy to discern that each of the three primary challenges driving nonprofit uncertainty—generational divide, polarization, and race—was at work here. (As was the problem of mission creep, an issue we will return to in Chapter 8.) Olderman's decisions were surely influenced by the reality that she is a Jewish woman leading an organization that primarily serves Black and Latino clients. Many of the people within Bronx Defenders clamoring to support the Palestinian cause were people of color who were younger and more radical than the organization's leadership. The entire affair raised the question of accountability. Who should Bronx Defenders be accountable to? The board that governs the agency? The clients who count on the agency for representation? The taxpayers and other funders who underwrite their services? The cause of social justice writ large?

According to Cass Sunstein, the author of *Conformity: The Power of Social Influences,* there is a natural tendency for groups of people to dwell on information that is shared by the majority of the group—and to ignore or avoid information that is possessed by only a few members of the group. This dynamic helps to fuel extremism. As Sunstein writes,

> With respect to information, the simple point is that people usually respond to the arguments made by other people—and the "argument pool," in any group with some initial disposition in one direction, will inevitably be skewed toward that disposition. A group whose members tend to think that Israel is the real aggressor in the Middle East conflict will tend to hear many arguments to that effect, and relatively few opposing views. It is almost inevitable that the group's members will have heard some, but not all, of the arguments that emerge from the discussion. Having heard all of what is said, people are likely to move further in the anti-Israel direction. So too with a group whose members tend to oppose immigration: group members will hear a large number of arguments against immigration and a smaller number of arguments on its behalf. If people are listening, they will have a stronger conviction, in line with the same view with which they began, as a result of deliberation.[7]

Note the irony here: we generally think of deliberation as a good thing, as a way to avoid rash decisions. But when an organization is ideologically homogeneous, deliberation doesn't play this function. Instead, it does essentially the opposite: winding people up toward a more extreme version of what they already believed and silencing anyone who disagrees. And this is how a mainstream opinion like "Hamas bears a lot of responsibility for the conflict in Israel"—a statement supported by 65% of Americans according to a Pew poll in December of 2023—becomes next to impossible to articulate within an organization like Bronx Defenders.[8]

A monoculture has emerged at too many nonprofit organizations—a monoculture that brooks no dissent from prevailing orthodoxy on a host of issues, including those, like the conflict in the Middle East, where there is spirited public debate and legitimate arguments to be made for many different positions.

It wasn't always thus. One former Bronx Defenders attorney told me, "Bronx Defenders was always pretty hardcore about representing their clients. What changed over the years, as the organization got bigger and younger and the union came in, is that it started to get pretty hardcore about a lot of other stuff too." According to criminal-defense attorney and blogger Scott Greenfield,

> Over the past decade, public defenders' offices, at least in New York, have become increasingly dedicated to social justice. While the lawyers who took on the representation of the indigent always trended to the left, the offices became increasingly progressive rather than liberal, and increasingly intolerant of anyone who wasn't dedicated to the farthest left fashions. More than a few of the long-time public defenders have told me that if they applied for a job today, they wouldn't get it because they were insufficiently woke. They say it as if it's a joke, but it's no joke. They live in fear of the younger lawyers, who will attack them at the slightest hint of heresy.[9]

This is an unhealthy state of affairs. As the case of Bronx Defenders illustrates, belief polarization can fundamentally alter the culture of an agency, hampering external communications, threatening organizational legitimacy, and undermining the ability to recruit and retain talented staff.

ASSOCIATIONS WITHOUT MEMBERS

Ideally, American nonprofits should be part of the answer to polarization. And, in fairness, many are currently performing exactly this function. Particularly at the local level, there are thousands of nonprofit groups that are bringing people together, regardless of their political orientation, to address neighborhood problems and to make their community a better place to live.

But a significant subset of the nonprofit sector is actively pushing in the other direction. Sometimes intentionally and sometimes by accident, these organizations (and the foundations and individual donors that support them) are promoting political polarization in the United States. On both the right and the left, there are numerous think tanks, advocacy groups, impact litigation firms, and nonprofit media organizations that are dedicated to pursuing highly ideological goals.

While nonprofits are prohibited from playing a direct role in advancing political candidates if they want to maintain their tax-exempt status, many engage in work that is frankly political in nature. In the process, they play an outsized role in shaping our national conversation.

Nonprofits have a long history of influencing policy debates in the United States, of course—groups like the ACLU and the NAACP have been major players in American politics for 100 years or more.

But a big change took place starting in the 1960s. Before then, large membership organizations with dozens of local branches used to be a regular feature of American civic life. Groups like the Masons, Lions, American Legion, League of Women Voters, and Daughters of the American Revolution used to be some of the most prominent organizations in the country.

Today, many of the most influential nonprofits do not have significant membership rolls. Their direction is determined not by volunteers but by well-paid professionals. Many of these organizations are based in Washington, DC; focused on federal policy; and backed by large foundation grants. Harvard University sociologist Theda Skocpal calls these groups "associations without members."

There are definitely upsides to associations without members. Memberless organizations are likely to be easier to manage and quicker on their feet. But something has been lost too. The membership associations were places that engaged millions of Americans, often across lines of class and ideology. (They were, to be fair, less likely to be open to Americans of all races and sexual orientations, which is one reason why many of them have fallen into eclipse.)

Robert Putnam, the author of *Bowling Alone*, has written persuasively about the collapse of American community as people have abandoned the kinds of civic organizations that used to bind us together. In a similar vein, Skocpal declares that "the old civic America has been bypassed and shoved to the side by a gaggle of professionally dominated advocacy groups and nonprofit institutions rarely attached to memberships worthy of the name. Ideals of shared citizenship and possibilities for democratic leverage have been compromised in the process."[10]

The shift to professionally dominated nonprofit groups may not be one of the main drivers of polarization in the United States, but it has certainly been a contributing force. According to Steven Teles, a professor of political science at Johns Hopkins University,

> You've got what I've called "advocacy" rather than representation, in which groups claim to speak for constituencies that they don't actually have any organic structures of

> accountability to. I think that has had some important impacts on both the left and right. On the left, it has simultaneously encouraged an embrace of positions on social issues that are not widely supported by the actual people being advocated for, but also a kind of piecemeal, bite-sized economic policy that flows out of the fact that they are not trying to organize mass constituencies. On the right, I think it encouraged an economic policy that was at odds with the actual preferences of conservative voters (but aligned with conservative donors, whose preferences ran strongly libertarian on economics) on things like entitlements and trade. One way to think about the politics of the last few decades is that we've had an ideological conflict on both social and economic issues as a consequence of the incentives of the organizations competing for attention; that has left broad swathes of what the public actually cares about relatively unorganized.[11]

In 2020, Alexander C. Furnas, a professor at Northwestern University, and Tim LaPira, a professor at James Madison University, surveyed over 3,500 political elites—defined as "those who hold significant authoritative roles in government, or those outside government whose occupations position them to influence those inside government," including nonprofit leaders. They compared the responses of their elite sample to the opinions of likely voters on a host of policy issues. They found that both Democratic and Republican elites were more ideological than likely voters—Republican elites were more right-wing and Democratic elites were more left-wing.[12]

Nonprofit organizations don't need to align perfectly with the opinions of the general public, of course. Some nonprofits should be cutting-edge actors, testing ideas that have little public support. But we may have reached some sort of invisible tipping point where there are too many nonprofits acting in too nakedly an ideological fashion.

As the Introduction highlighted, trust is the lubricant that allows the nonprofit sector to function smoothly, enabling organizations to recruit staff, volunteers, donors, and other partners. Unfortunately, public confidence in the sector is shrinking. According to Dan Cardinali, the former head of the Independent Sector,

> [a] major reason why trust in civil society is diminishing is the sharp increase in political and cultural polarization. Rather than seeking commonalities with their neighbors, Americans are self-selecting into communities that reinforce existing viewpoints, interests, and beliefs. . . . America has always been a nation of rich differences. Over the last 30 years, however, [a] "great sort" has eroded our connection to those who diverge from our beliefs, experiences, and worldview. As a result, private action on behalf of the public good is increasingly circumscribed by what one considers her or his community. When community is limited to those with whom you share a worldview, then American civil society is deeply compromised in its ability to build a common good that extends beyond any limited, self-selected group.[13]

We should seek to avoid a future where nonprofits are divided into those that serve conservatives and those that serve progressives. But in our over-politicized era, all too many nonprofits are effectively performing exactly this kind of sorting with the kind of language they use to describe their work.

Pick a few nonprofits at random and take a look at their mission statements. If you see words like "freedom" and "prosperity" and "opportunity" (to say nothing of "law and order" or "American dream"), you'll know that you are looking at an organization that is attempting to signal its conservative bona fides. Words like "equity," "Latinx," and "structural racism" perform the same work in the opposite direction.

The idea of persuasion seems to have fallen out of favor—many organizations aren't even trying to speak to people who don't already agree with them. The underlying message that this sends to people on the other side of any given issue is, if not outright contempt, then utter indifference at the very least.

THE WORK IS MORE IMPORTANT THAN THE WORDS

As if using ideologically freighted language weren't signal enough, in recent years many nonprofits have further communicated their political orientation by issuing public statements in response to current events. This issue has played out most visibly on American campuses. In the wake of George Floyd, hundreds of colleges issued statements declaring their solidarity with Black Lives Matter. In subsequent months, a range of other events also elicited statements, including the war in Ukraine, the Supreme Court's abortion decision in *Dobbs v. Jackson*, and various mass shootings.

And then came October 7, 2023.

In the aftermath of Hamas's attack on Israel, many Jewish students and organizations expected to see statements of solidarity similar to those issued in the wake of George Floyd's killing. When they did not immediately appear, or were issued using language viewed as tepid, the fallout was intense: cue student complaints, trustee resignations, alumni protest campaigns, and even congressional hearings.

The reverberations of this controversy will continue to linger for some time, but one potentially positive result is that it will encourage many places to get out of the business of issuing statements. In an open letter, three free-speech organizations—The Academic Freedom Alliance, Heterodox Academy, and the Foundation for Individual Rights and Expression—called on universities to abandon the practice and embrace "institutional neutrality" instead. "In recent years," the letter argues, "colleges and universities have increasingly weighed in on social and political issues. This has led our institutions of higher education to become politicized and has created an untenable situation whereby they are expected to weigh in on all social and political issues. Most critically, these stances risk establishing an orthodox view on campus, threatening the pursuit of knowledge for which higher education exists."[14]

The push for institutional neutrality has not yet migrated beyond academia and into the larger nonprofit universe. But there are signs that some nonprofits outside of the ivory tower are starting to recalibrate their public communications. I talked to the leader of one national nonprofit that had loudly proclaimed its solidarity with the Black Lives Matter movement and highlighted the organization's commitment to racial justice on its website in 2020. "With the benefit of hindsight, we maybe over-swung a little on our messaging," she now admits.

This became an issue when some of the organization's government partners objected to the use of language like "anti-racist" on their website. In response, the organization did something unusual: They gathered everyone who was working on the project and explained that the organization's ongoing work was being jeopardized by this vocabulary. The matter was ultimately put to a team discussion. "As an organization, we remain committed to racial justice," the executive explained to me, "but the results were nearly unanimous: our team agreed that the work is more important than the words. It is crucial that we be able to work in both blue states and red states."

This story illustrates two of the underlying themes of this book. First, it is an example of a brand of leadership that looks to engage in democratic decision-making where possible, allowing dissenters to voice their opinions and widening the circle of people who feel like they have a stake in what happens to the organization. Just as important, this is a case study of prioritizing impact over symbols and the mission of an organization over the feelings of staff members. This won't be the last time these two notes appear in these pages.

Chapter 4

The Rise and Fall (and Rise Again?) of DEI

A couple of years before Covid hit, I went to a training on how to advance "anti-racism" within my organization. The training was convened by a prominent local foundation and was expressly targeted to nonprofit executives.

If I'm honest, I would say that I didn't really want to go to the training; I was cajoled into attending by a committee that I had convened to study racial justice issues within the Center for Court Innovation. At that point, we were still a few years away from the kinds of staff upheavals that have since torn apart many nonprofits, but even back then you could feel things percolating. I was trying to figure out how to manage a rapidly shifting environment, where more and more staffers seemed to expect their agency to boldly advocate for social and racial justice, both internally and externally.

The training was not horrible. Certainly, it did not conform to the anti-woke caricature of diversity trainings. There were no rituals of self-abasement. I wasn't asked to confess my sins. I never felt like I was participating in an indoctrination session or a cult meeting.

The basic thrust of the training was that "equity" should be a leader's overriding concern in managing a nonprofit organization. What that meant was taking pains to ensure that Black staffers (as well as members of other minority groups) received their due. There was little or no acknowledgment that agencies could have other, and perhaps conflicting, north stars, such as delivering excellent service to clients or solving difficult social problems.

Throughout the day-long training, there was much talk about how to create organizational cultures in which everyone felt "seen" and could "bring their whole selves to work." The trainers wanted us to devote time, energy, and money toward ensuring that all staffers could succeed within our organizations.

At some abstract level, this goal seems unobjectionable to me, but I felt then (and still feel today) that it is in tension with some of the day-to-day realities of managing an institution, which always involves trade-offs, competing priorities, and limited resources.

Toward the end of the training, I raised my hand. "Isn't our job as leaders, at some level, to pick winners and losers?" I asked. "If we have a big job opening, we don't hire everyone who applies for the position. We choose the person we think would be best for the job, and we deliver bad news to the rest of the applicants. In lots of situations, everyone can't succeed at the same time."

I must admit I was deliberately being a little provocative—I knew that using terms like "winners" and "losers" would be jarring to many of my fellow nonprofit executives, to say nothing of the trainers.

I'm glad to say that no one fainted. I wasn't thrown out of the training. But it was clear that I had said something that was contrary to the whole spirit of the enterprise.

I left the training feeling out of step with the other nonprofit leaders in the room. I also left feeling deeply ambivalent. The training was better than I had feared. It had none of the hallmarks of a struggle session and it focused attention on the importance of fairness and staff happiness, which I believe are important to the health of any organization. On the other hand, I felt the training took its case too far, suggesting that all other organizational values and aspirations should be subservient to the goals of diversity, equity, and inclusion.

***

The murder of George Floyd in 2020 and all that took place afterward—the heartfelt protests and the chaos in the streets and the anguish on social media and so much more besides—was a signal moment in the life of American nonprofits. It will no doubt continue to reverberate for years to come.

In many respects, 2020 serves as a dividing line for the American nonprofit sector. In the days that followed, many of the old norms were dispensed with and new ways of doing business put in their place.

The most obvious change was that it seemed like almost every nonprofit, more or less overnight, decided that they were a racial justice organization. Agency after agency affirmed their solidarity with Black Lives Matter, declared their opposition to racism, and pledged to do better.

But this presented a conundrum: What did it mean to do better? How could nonprofits make tangible their commitment to the cause? Clearly just issuing statements was not enough.

The answer, for many organizations, was committing to diversity, equity, and inclusion, or DEI. While every nonprofit seemed to mouth the same language, repeating "diversity, equity, and inclusion" like an incantation, the meaning of these words proved maddeningly elusive.

At first, the branding seemed a stroke of brilliance. Who could be against diversity, equity, and inclusion? If the words didn't quite evoke the same warm feelings as "mom and apple pie," they were at least vague enough not to provoke immediate opposition.

Functionally, the American nonprofit embrace of DEI tended to focus on three activities: internal reflection, training, and hiring/promotion. An entire industry of consultants, many of them quite expensive, came into existence to help nonprofits with these things. (McKinsey & Company has estimated that $8 billion annually is spent on diversity trainings alone.)[1] In the years following 2020, it was difficult to find nonprofits that weren't engaging expensive consultants and newly hired senior administrators to help them facilitate soul-searching sessions, conduct anti-bias workshops, and rethink how they selected and promoted staff. It seemed like DEI would be a growth industry for a generation to come.

That was then.

Today, "diversity, equity, and inclusion" reads very differently. These are no longer anodyne concepts—these are now fighting words. A powerful DEI backlash has emerged that shows little sign of abating soon. One of Donald Trump's first acts, upon returning to office in 2025, was to issue a series of executive orders targeting federal DEI initiatives. Trump's orders didn't come out of the blue—they were the culmination of years of concerted work designed to roll back DEI. Multiple states have passed legislation signaling their opposition to DEI. The Supreme Court ruled against Harvard in a case widely viewed as a major blow for affirmative action. Public universities in Kentucky and Nebraska have eliminated their DEI offices. Many corporations have begun to eliminate DEI jobs. "DEI Goes Quiet," a 2024 *New York Times* headline announced.[2]

Some of this is the work of right-wing activists like Christopher Rufo, who has launched well-orchestrated campaigns against DEI and identity politics generally. But some of the backlash to DEI has been an organic reaction to what many people—right, left, and center—have come to feel are the mistakes, injustices, and overreach of DEI programs.

Before we look at what has gone wrong with DEI, it is important to underline again that there are good reasons why critics have demanded that nonprofits pay more attention to issues of race and fairness. The sector has a long history of tyrannical executives, many of whom have remained in place for decades, impossible to dislodge from their seats of power. A great many of these executives are white, as are the members of their boards and their senior teams. There's nothing wrong with the desire to diversify nonprofits and to see new faces in leadership positions.

Junior staffers at nonprofits are often the ones actively demanding greater investment in DEI. A 2022 survey found that 72% of workers under the age of 35 said that they would consider turning down a job offer or leaving their company if they thought their manager did not support DEI initiatives.[3] Nonprofit leaders cannot just ignore these kinds of findings. Seen from one perspective, DEI is simply good business, a way to demonstrate to staffers from diverse backgrounds—who can always take their labor to other places if they so choose—that their employer cares about them and wants to build a healthy organizational culture.

Many nonprofit leaders report that they have seen their investments in DEI pay off. As the executive director of one nonprofit in New York City told me, "Nonprofits are seeing a tangible return on investment on their DEI efforts through increased employee and community member engagement, satisfaction, and retention." Another executive director concurred: "DEI helps encourage participation at all levels of an agency because it allows staff to give voice to something everyone shares—personal experiences, background, and culture. When done well, DEI improves internal communications."[4]

In an increasingly heterogeneous country, it is essential that we create nonprofit organizations that can attract diverse talent, get them to work together effectively, and treat them fairly. To the extent that DEI programs have helped organizations move toward these goals, they should be celebrated.

Unfortunately, as is often the case, the devil is in the details.

THE CASE OF FRAN ITKOFF

Fran Itkoff was 90 years old when she found herself at the center of a social media firestorm.

For 60 years (!), Itkoff had volunteered for the National Multiple Sclerosis Society in California. Her interest in MS was deeply personal: her husband was diagnosed with MS before he passed away.

Despite her decades of service, in 2024 Itkoff was asked by the National MS Society to stop her work as a volunteer. The reason? Itkoff didn't understand why people were listing their pronouns on letters and had asked someone at the MS Society what it all meant. According to the MS Society, Itkoff's statement did not align with their DEI policy, so she was effectively terminated.

The story was picked up by Libs of TikTok, the account of a right-wing provocateur who highlights examples of woke excess, and then it ricocheted around the Internet. What followed had the feeling of inevitability: hundreds of angry people online bewailing what had happened and the National MS Society quickly apologizing in an effort to put the whole controversy behind them.

The "firing" of Fran Itkoff resonated the way it did because it seemed emblematic of larger failings of the DEI movement. As *Inc.* explained, the National MS Society seemed to make a mockery of the values of diversity, equity, and inclusion: "If you value diversity, you need to accept that people are different and that's OK. If you value equity, being fair and impartial means you have to acknowledge that people come from different positions, which doesn't mean they are inherently bad. And inclusion? If you are trying to keep marginalized people from being excluded, excluding a 90-year-old is really not the look that you want."[5]

This has been a recurring theme in the growing opposition to DEI: the sense that a movement that on its face seems to promote tolerance is actually fundamentally intolerant, demanding adherence to a set of political ideas, and an arcane vocabulary, that not everyone shares.

Is DEI an ideological project? Yes, says Christopher Rufo of the Manhattan Institute: "DEI employs a propagandistic language to conceal its real intentions. It is, in fact, the opposite of what it appears to be."[6] As Rufo knows, there is a deep strain of cultural conservatism in the United States. According to *Compact* magazine, this brand of conservatism is marked by

> Frustration with speech codes and an HR mentality seen as making America oversensitive, unfun, insipid, preachy; by opposition to cancel culture; by a dislike of DEI and diversity mandates . . . ; by a mistrust of the bureaucratic elements of society and government; by a perception that the epistemic institutions of our society (the media, academia, NGOs, and so forth) are incompetent and biased; and by an antipathy toward the invasive and moralizing tendencies of "woke" social movements.[7]

In recent years, cultural conservatives have successfully turned "DEI" into an epithet, for example labeling Vice President Kamala Harris a "DEI hire." According to *The Guardian*, DEI has become "the latest dog-whistle term in the conservative war of words to frame basic egalitarianism as a net negative."[8]

But in truth it is not just right-wing activists who have been asking hard questions about DEI. Increasingly, liberals and moderates have also started to express doubts about DEI. DEI has been hemorrhaging support for a variety of reasons, including:

The Jewish challenge: In the wake of the war in Gaza, a wave of protests hit American educational and cultural institutions as pro-Palestinian activists attempted to argue for a ceasefire and divestment from Israel. Many Jewish students complained that these protests engaged in rhetoric and behavior that made them feel unsafe. In the past, universities had explicitly sought to police "microaggressions" and responded swiftly when members of other minority groups made claims of bias or harassment. The failure of Harvard, Columbia, and other high-profile institutions to act with the same alacrity when Jewish students were alleging victimization has led many to conclude that there are different standards for Jews. "As a practical matter . . . DEI programs limit their 'equity' and 'inclusion' efforts to certain identity groups, which rarely include Jews," says Tammi Rossman-Benjamin, the director of a nonprofit dedicated to combatting antisemitism.[9]

In a similar vein, Bari Weiss, writing in *Tablet*, makes the case that the DEI worldview, which typically argues that racial and ethnic groups should be represented within any American organization or field of endeavor in accordance to their percentage of the national population, poses a unique threat to Jews: "If underrepresentation is the inevitable outcome of systemic bias, then overrepresentation—and Jews are 2% of the American population—suggests not talent or hard work, but unearned privilege."[10] Weiss reaches a stark conclusion: it is time, she believes, to "end DEI."

Racial affinity groups: In an effort to create a welcoming environment, many organizations have created special spaces for members of traditionally marginalized groups. This can include hosting separate lounges, affinity groups, or Slack channels. The idea makes a certain amount of sense: it can sometimes be stressful to be a visible minority and it can often be helpful to compare notes with others who are going through similar experiences. Some schools have even created separate classes that are only open to Black and Latino students.

These kinds of developments have raised hackles for obvious reasons. It would appear that, in the name of combatting racism, some organizations are advancing a version of racial segregation. In 2023, the US Department of Education weighed in on such efforts, issuing guidance that schools cannot create groups that exclude students on the basis of race, even in the name of fighting racism.

Despite this guidance, many workplaces continue to convene separate caucuses and training sessions for different racial and ethnic groups. These efforts will always be susceptible to claims of segregation. "Segregation in the form of racial affinity groups today is disturbingly similar in concept to the separate bathrooms, water fountains, bus sections, and other spaces in generations past," writes Joseph Klein for the Foundation Against Intolerance and Racism. "Then as now, we ought to remember the world-changing verdict from Brown v. Board of Education, that 'Separate [is] inherently unequal.'"[11]

"White supremacy culture": Back in the 1990s, a diversity consultant named Tema Okun attempted to define what she called "white supremacy culture." Some of the characteristics of white supremacy, according to Okun, included a sense of urgency, worship of the written word, individualism, and objectivity.[12] Although Okun admits that the article she wrote was "not researched," her ideas have traveled far and wide—organizations across the country have used or adapted Okun's work in the years since she came up with it.[13]

When the National Museum of African American History and Culture posted a similar list, defining attributes like "hard work" and "rational thinking" as aspects of white culture, it was widely condemned, with many critics pointing out that the list's underlying assumptions perversely mirrored those of white nationalists. Under duress, the museum ended up issuing an apology (although it was pretty half-hearted). Reviewing the controversy, Robert Tracinski, writing for *The Bulwark*, concluded, "the harder you try to be 'progressive,' by today's standards, the closer you get to the alt-right."[14]

Viewpoint diversity: This is the typical way that a nonprofit will define "diversity" in an organizational DEI statement: "Diversity refers to race, gender, ethnicity, nationality, religion, sexual identity, familial status, age, disability and socio-economic status." Notably absent from this lengthy list is any mention of different kinds of ideological or cultural viewpoints. Nor is there any reference to military veterans, levels of educational attainment or other forms of difference that would signify a broader conception of the meaning of diversity. Given this oversight, it is understandable why many critics have concluded that nonprofits that embrace DEI are not in fact welcoming places for a broad array of political perspectives. "If other people matter, then so do their viewpoints," argues educator Erin McLaughlin.[15]

Viewpoint diversity became a national talking point in the spring of 2024 when Uri Berliner, an editor at National Public Radio, accused the national nonprofit of bias against ideas that didn't conform to left-wing orthodoxy. Writing in *The Free Press*, Berliner argued that "An open-minded spirit no longer exists within NPR, and now, predictably, we don't have an audience that reflects America."[16] After trying for years without success to get higher-ups to hear his concerns, Berliner ultimately left the network.

There is little doubt that a similar dynamic holds sway at many other nonprofits, with those who don't share the dominant politics feeling increasingly unwelcome. As Helen Pluckrose, the co-author of *Cynical Theories*, has said, "When diversity is just about people with different identities who all believe the same thing, then diversity training can often look a lot more like conformity training."[17]

***

All of these issues are red meat for the attack dogs of the culture wars. Nonprofit DEI programs that endorse or engage in these practices have received significant pushback from unhappy staff, disgruntled donors, and skeptical external critics.

But culture war issues are just one of many threats to DEI. Another major vulnerability is a lack of evidence: there is very little research that suggests that diversity training in particular makes a difference.

A REVOLUTION OF THE MIND?

As Elisabeth Lasch-Quinn details in the provocative (and persuasive) *Race Experts: How Racial Etiquette, Sensitivity Training and*

New Age Therapy Hijacked the Civil Rights Revolution, diversity training has been around for generations, emerging from the ashes of the civil rights movement. According to Lasch-Quinn, diversity training is the red-headed stepchild of two American obsessions: race and self-help.

Lasch-Quinn bemoans the rise of "etiquette advisers and diversity trainers" who use "New Age therapies" like sensitivity training and encounter groups to pursue a dubious "revolution of the mind." She sees this development as nothing short of tragedy:

> Out of the maelstrom of the 1960s rose an army of race experts whose ministrations unintentionally helped prolong old racial tensions and foster new misunderstandings and anxieties. The interpretations of our racial situation offered by these experts stand in the way of our adjustment to an integrated America.... The world of the diversity engineers is a world in which virulent white racism and white supremacist attitudes still reign unchallenged, a world of victims and victimizers, a world in perpetual recovery, a world of endless slights. Here racist crimes and social faux pas are one and the same—all inspired by a monolithic, unabated white racial hatred. All whites must confess to their inherent racism, or they are, in the words of the recovery movement, "in denial."[18]

Of course, there is no government agency that certifies diversity trainers, so standards and approaches vary widely. Some trainers focus on implicit bias. Some narrowly instruct participants how to conform with the law. Others are designed to heighten sensitivity to different cultures. And some offer a more radical, "anti-oppression" lens that attempts to enlist people in the fight to end white supremacy.

Given all of the different approaches, it is difficult to offer a definitive judgment on the efficacy of diversity training. Still, what we do know is not encouraging. "There are dozens, if not hundreds, of studies, most of them showing that diversity training has no effects," says Alexandra Kalev, an associate professor at Tel Aviv University and coauthor of *Getting to Diversity*. According to Kalev,

> What we've learned is that it's very hard for people to be forced to change their attitudes. . . . We've learned that trying to suppress stereotypes makes those stereotypes more accessible. We've learned that the message of multiculturalism makes white men feel excluded. And when it comes to attitudes, we gain them through the life course, so no single afternoon session will undo that.[19]

Kalev's opinion is hardly an outlier. In "Diversity Training Goals, Limitations, and Promise: A Review of the Multidisciplinary Literature," published in the *Annual Review of Psychology 2022*, professors Patricia Devine and Tory Ash look at the results of dozens of studies of diversity training in organizational settings. They identify a major flaw that mars the field. Although many diversity training programs seek to address systemic problems like workplace discrimination, the failure to attract and retain employees from various minority groups, and the lack of diversity in upper management, researchers are rarely able to measure these kinds of outcomes. Instead, they tend to assess diversity trainings at the level of the individual, asking participants whether they got value out of the experience and whether their attitudes have changed. There is a clear disconnect between these kinds of individual impacts and the larger goals that diversity trainings seek to achieve.

Devine and Ash went into their review hoping to identify and share best practices in diversity training. By the end of their research, they reluctantly conclude that they cannot do so. They report their findings with an almost audible sigh:

> Unfortunately, our primary conclusion following our review of the recent literature echoes that of scholars who conducted reviews of the diversity training literature in the past. Despite multidisciplinary endorsement of the practice of diversity training, we are far from being able to derive clear and decisive conclusions about what fosters inclusivity and promotes diversity within organizations. This state of affairs is concerning, particularly in light of the enthusiasm for, and monetary investment in, diversity training. Implementation of diversity training has clearly outpaced the available evidence that such programs are effective in achieving their goals.[20]

Despite these kinds of findings, nonprofit organizations across the country continue to invest in diversity trainings. Some are simply ignorant of the research. Some are no doubt using the trainings cynically, to stave off more significant change agendas. But probably most of the nonprofit leaders who continue to pay good money to diversity trainers are doing so out of sheer desperation. They want to signal that they care about pursuing racial justice and addressing the grievances of their teams. Diversity trainings, for all their flaws, are a visible symbol that an organization values such things. But they will become harder and harder to defend as the word continues to spread about their lack of results.

"BLACK TALENT AND OTHERS"

Central to many organizational DEI programs is an effort to hire, retain, and promote greater numbers of Black Americans, along with members of other traditionally marginalized groups. This is a laudable goal, and there are many approaches to achieving it. Few reasonable people would argue against attempting to cast a wider net for job applicants or creating links between employers and historically black universities or rethinking degree requirements for certain kinds of positions.

But many nonprofits have gone well beyond these kinds of efforts in their quest for diversity. This includes embracing "race conscious" internships, fellowships, grant programs and more. Ironically, these efforts create a real risk for institutional DEI programs because, depending upon the framing and execution, they may be in violation of federal civil rights legislation. According to Title VII of the Civil Rights Act, it is illegal to consider a candidate's race in employment decisions, even if an employer is motivated by a desire to create a more diverse workforce.

In recent years, two important warning shots have been fired across the bow of the nonprofit sector. The first was the Supreme Court's ruling in the *Students for Fair Admissions v. Harvard* case. The Court held that Harvard had discriminated against Asian American applicants to the college, in violation of the Civil Rights Act of 1964. This effectively means that affirmative action, as practiced by Harvard and many other colleges, has been declared illegal.

While the Supreme Court's decision was confined to higher education, many grantmakers, businesses, and nonprofits understood that they could be the next ones to face a lawsuit alleging this kind of systematic discrimination. In 2024, the other shoe dropped for the Fearless Fund, an Atlanta grant program designed to aid Black women business owners. The case against the Fearless Fund was brought by the American Alliance for Equal Rights, a group led by Edward Blum, the same conservative activist who was also behind the Harvard admissions case. A federal appeals court ordered the Fearless Fund to suspend its grant contest, which provides $20,000 to businesses that are owned by Black women. Further litigation on these kinds of issues is all but inevitable, and another Supreme Court case seems likely.

Some nonprofit organizations will no doubt continue to engage in race-conscious policies and practices, hoping that no aggrieved party will sue them or that they will receive a favorable hearing in court. But many organizations will understandably be unwilling to take that kind of a risk—defending a lawsuit can be an expensive proposition and submitting to discovery can require the airing of a lot of dirty laundry.

There are signs that some organizations are beginning to adapt to the new world order. One example is OneTen, a nonprofit that was explicitly created in the wake of George Floyd's murder to lift one million Black workers into good-paying jobs. But in recent months, they have gotten the message that Black-only hiring programs are a potential magnet for lawsuits. The organization has now modified its messaging, emphasizing that it seeks to help "Black talent and others."[21] We will likely see many organizations follow this lead in the days to come.

WHERE DO WE GO FROM HERE?

It would be a tragic mistake for nonprofits to give up on the core goals of DEI programs. But it would be sheer folly to continue to insist on vocabulary that has become politically polarizing and approaches that can show little evidence of efficacy and run a demonstrable risk of violating civil rights law.

What's a nonprofit leader to do? First, they would be well-advised to rebrand their organization's DEI work to send a strong signal that a new day has dawned. Monica Harris, the executive director of the Foundation Against Intolerance and Racism agrees. "The greatest danger I see is that the DEI branding threatens to undermine all diversity," she told me. "And diversity is the lifeblood of this country." In particular, Harris finds "equity" a troubling concept:

> I think "equity," in a vacuum, means justice and fairness. But the way it's being construed now is a very distorted interpretation of equity that essentially means that in order for some people to have more, or in order for some people to succeed, others must be brought down. It's a sort of leveling, of bringing people down to the lowest common denominator. And it doesn't allow for excellence. And it doesn't reward the ambitious. And I think that those are part and parcel of the American experience. So equity to me is antithetical to everything America stands for.[22]

In *The Identity Trap*, Yascha Mounk argues that many recent "race-sensitive" policies and programs, including racial affinity groups, are counter-productive. Indeed, he suggests that these developments fly in the face of social science. Citing the work of psychologist Gordon Allport, Mounk makes the case that a key weapon in the fight against prejudice is intergroup contact. The research suggests that people in integrated housing tend to have less biased views than those who live in segregated living situations, for example.

But in order for intergroup contact to work its magic, certain prerequisites must be in place. Members of different groups must have basically equal status (for example, interacting with one another as teammates). They must have a common goal that requires cooperation. And their efforts must be supported by the relevant authority figures (say, their coach). "By contrast," Mounk writes, the kinds of "rules and rituals" that are being put in place in many American institutions seem "custom designed to minimize the promise of greater mutual understanding through intergroup contact because they directly violate the conditions discovered by Allport and his followers."[23]

Following this line of thinking, nonprofits might consider engaging their staff members in community service projects and other activities that flatten hierarchy and necessitate teamwork without any explicit racial agenda. According to novelist Aldous Huxley, "Happiness is not achieved by the conscious pursuit of happiness; it is generally the byproduct of other activities." At least some of the goals of DEI programs, like reducing interpersonal bias, are probably better achieved indirectly than directly.

Frank Dobbin and Alexandra Kalev, the authors of *Getting to Diversity,* suggest that a big part of the problem with current DEI efforts is the use of mandatory trainings. The conventional wisdom has been that the best way to signal that an organization is serious about diversity is to force all employees to participate in training sessions on the topic. Dobbin and Kalev argue that this approach backfires: "People often respond to compulsory courses with anger and resistance—and many participants actually report more animosity toward other groups afterward. But voluntary training evokes the opposite response ('I chose to show up, so I must be pro-diversity'), leading to better results."[24]

Dobbin and Kalev also believe that mentoring is crucial to achieving organizational diversity goals. Mentoring can be an important tool for both mentors and mentees. For mentees, it can obviously help expand career horizons and create valuable connections up the organizational chain. For mentors, the relationship can help them understand in a more intimate way some of the barriers that people of color and other minority groups face as they attempt to navigate their careers. (We will return to the subject of mentoring in some depth in Chapter 7.)

These ideas just scratch the surface. As it becomes increasingly clear that the current DEI model is toxic, many people who are committed to American diversity have begun searching for a better paradigm. According to *New York Times* columnist David Brooks, "The right intellectual framework for effective diversity work is pluralism. Pluralism starts with a celebration of the fact that we live in one of the most diverse societies in history. . . . Pluralists seek to replace the demonizing, demeaning and dividing ethos with one that encourages respect, relationships and cooperation. Pluralists believe that people's identities are complex and shifting, that most human beings shouldn't be divided into good/evil categories, that we become wise as we enter into many different points of view."[25]

Brooks is hardly the only important voice endorsing pluralism. In recent years, a number of new philanthropic and community-building initiatives have emerged under this banner, attracting support across a pretty broad ideological spectrum. For example, in April 2023, a group of funders wrote an op-ed in the *Chronicle of Philanthropy* endorsing philanthropic pluralism. The co-authors included the leaders of the Ford Foundation and the Koch Brothers foundation (Stand Together)—unusual bedfellows indeed.

While the op-ed did not focus explicitly on DEI, it attempted to push back, ever so gently, against ideological conformity:

> Some of the stress on pluralism is stylistic, but much is substantive. Many of the issues that divide America are real and consequential. When it comes to issues such as race, wealth, climate, and religion, the stakes are high. And as the stakes grow, so too do the perceived costs of engagement—or even toleration—of people, views, and ideas on the other side of ever brighter lines of division. The result of these pressures, however meritorious and morally urgent, is that foundations and philanthropists are often expected to pledge allegiance to one or another narrow set of prescribed views.[26]

It is perhaps a sign of the times that even this carefully worded, written-so-as-not-to-offend statement was immediately attacked by critics on both the left and the right. The sad truth is that many prominent people have a personal and institutional stake in sustaining our current era of polarization. This includes, most obviously, President Trump, who sees an opportunity to energize his base and "own the libs" by attacking DEI programs.

In the face of Trump's relentless provocation, many advocates of American diversity are choosing to dig in their heels and fight like hell to protect the status quo practice of DEI in government, businesses, and nonprofits. This is an understandable response to aggression. It is also exactly what Trump wants.

At the risk of cliché, a moment of crisis can also be a window of opportunity. Hopefully in the days to come we will see a thousand flowers bloom as nonprofits experiment with new ways to achieve and embrace diversity.

The battle to create a nonprofit sector where everyone feels welcome and where leadership reflects the diversity of the country is still very much ongoing. Even as nonprofits adapt to changing conditions on the ground, it is important to also acknowledge that significant progress has been made. The executive ranks of nonprofits are demonstrably more diverse today than they were when I first got started in the early 1990s. A recent survey of more than 45,000 nonprofits suggests that 15% of CEOs now identify as Black.[27] This is a healthy sign that, over time, the nonprofit sector is capable of reforming itself.

PART II

A WAY THROUGH

Chapter 5

Good Stewardship

In *The Great Experiment: Why Diverse Democracies Fall Apart and How They Can Endure,* Yascha Mounk identifies a problem that is common to many books about social issues:

> Books about big ideas often suffer from a serious flaw. In their first nine chapters, they identify a fascinating problem or challenge. They explain its causes and context. They show why it is worth worrying about and urgently needs to be solved. But any problem that is big and important enough that someone can write an interesting book about it is unlikely to be solved soon. And so the tenth chapter of these books is nearly always far less satisfying. Either it suggests huge changes of public policy or collective behavior that really would solve the problem—but are highly unrealistic. Or it suggests technical policy fixes or small adjustments in our lives that might actually be achievable—but will at best make a small difference.[1]

In writing this book, I wanted to avoid the Chapter 10 problem. I didn't want to spend 90% of my time describing the problems that nonprofits face and leave the potential solutions to a single, insufficient chapter at the end. So now we turn to the need for action. What should nonprofit leaders actually do? Is it possible to restore public confidence in nonprofits? And what kind of leadership will be required to make this happen?

***

Maurice Mitchell, the national director of the Working Families Party, has spent his entire career working for progressive causes. He defines himself as "a community organizer for racial, social and economic justice" and a leader in the Black Lives Matter movement.[2] He is neither a gadfly nor a social critic. So when Mitchell published "Building Resilient Organizations" on the internet at the end of 2022, it came out of the blue. Despite its bland title, the piece is a lacerating account of life within progressive nonprofit organizations. According to Mitchell,

> Executives in professional social justice institutions, grassroots activists in local movements, and fiery young radicals on protest lines are all advancing urgent concerns about the internal workings of progressive spaces. The themes arising are surprisingly consistent. Many claim that our spaces are "toxic" or "problematic," often sharing compelling and troubling personal anecdotes as evidence of this. People in leadership are finding their roles untenable, claiming it is "impossible" to execute campaigns or saying they are in organizations that are "stuck."[3]

Mitchell goes on to bemoan the "overidealistic demands," "reflexively anti-leadership orientation," and "anti-institutional sentiment" that have undermined all too many nonprofit organizations in recent years. He acknowledges that, in many places, small internal power struggles have essentially ruptured institutions, sapping their ability to "wage the broader struggle."

Because Mitchell has significant credibility in progressive circles thanks to his history of activism, his diagnosis could not be dismissed as conservative or anti-woke scolding. His essay was shared broadly within the nonprofit sector and eventually made its way into the mainstream media, earning Mitchell favorable coverage in the *New York Times*, MSNBC, and other outlets.

Mitchell's essay identifies a set of problems that are eroding the effectiveness of the American nonprofit sector from within and placing new pressures on nonprofit executives. To succeed these days, nonprofit leaders must do more than just raise money, craft an organizational vision, and guide staff, board, and volunteers toward it. Nonprofit executives must also navigate the three challenges outlined in the first half of this book—polarization, the generational divide, and calls for racial justice.

To do so effectively means navigating a path between denial and overcorrection. Nonprofit leaders must avoid both knee-jerk capitulation to the demands of their most radical staffers and the kind of symbolic battles that can drain organizational energy and effectiveness. This patient, tactical approach to managing institutional tensions might seem cowardly and insufficient to anti-woke advocates and left-wing activists, both of whom seek the catharsis of confrontation. But leaders can only govern with the consent of the governed, and few people are interested in being martyrs for abstract causes like free speech or due process.

A KINDER, GENTLER MODEL

Writing about nonprofit leadership is a tricky thing. There is, of course, no single way to lead an organization. And the nonprofit sector is staggeringly diverse. What works for a neighborhood-based advocacy organization that relies primarily on volunteers will not work for a citywide health agency with thousands of employees. This presents real analytical challenges. A granular approach, diving deep into the experience of an effective leader of a grassroots organization, will offer little of value to those concerned with larger organizations, and vice versa. On the other hand, engaging in high-level abstraction—extolling the virtue of "effective communication" or "resilience," say—runs the risk of offering nothing to nobody.

This chapter, and the chapters that follow, seek to forge a middle path. My goal is to identify a set of practices that nonprofit leaders have used to good effect in recent years. This is not meant to be an exhaustive list, nor am I suggesting that every good leader has done all of the things described here. Indeed, you could probably do all of the things outlined in this book and still end up a failure—leadership is a subtle art that is deeply dependent upon context. So, caveat emptor: as is always the case with leadership advice, your mileage may vary.

That having been said, it has become clear that certain leadership styles are better suited to dealing with the kinds of challenges currently confronting American organizations than others. The hard-charging, hard-nosed style of organizational leadership embodied by successful corporate CEOs like General Electric's Jack Welch has always been an uncomfortable fit in the nonprofit sector. The challenges of the moment are pushing nonprofit leaders even further in a kinder and gentler direction.

The tough-love style of leadership which expects excellence as a matter of course and scorns pats on the back is unlikely to succeed in today's nonprofit organizations. Young people these days have grown up in a world of instant feedback online. They are used to being able to measure their beauty or popularity by collecting likes and retweets and swipes right. Leaders have little choice but to figure out how to work with this reality.

I do not seek to advance a novel theory of leadership. Everything I know about leadership is based on having worked within nonprofit agencies—first as a staff member and then eventually graduating to leadership positions. My real-world experience managing complicated organizations has made one thing abundantly clear: a command-and-control style of leadership does not make sense for the nonprofit sector. I believe that there is a better way of doing business that is less top-down and more inclusive.

When I was first named the executive director of the Center for Court Innovation, I used the occasion as an excuse to reach out to a number of nonprofit leaders that I admired. I would recommend doing something similar to any new executive—I learned an enormous amount from making myself vulnerable and asking for advice from those who had "been there and done that."

There was, however, one discordant note that came up in several of these conversations. On more than one occasion, my informal advisors told me that I had to "put my personal stamp" on the organization. According to this mode of thinking, the organization should serve as a vehicle for my ambitions and my agenda.

Even at the time, before I had served a day as a nonprofit CEO, this seemed backward to me. My experience in the years since has not changed my perspective. In my view, nonprofit leaders should sublimate their personal goals and ideas to the needs of their organization. For lack of a better term, I would call this approach "good stewardship."

At the risk of being lofty (or blasphemous), running an organization is a sacred trust. Executive directors are asked to guide and protect a valuable commodity—the health and reputation of their agency. It is a responsibility, and a burden, that each executive carries for a limited time and then passes on to the next person. Nonprofit organizations belong to no one, not even long-serving founders.

In an era defined by the culture wars, good stewardship requires four qualities in particular: emotional intelligence, flexibility, humility, and long-term thinking.

Emotional Intelligence

Young people are coming into the workplace with different sensibilities, expectations, and needs than their predecessors. Managing Gen-Z and Millennial staffers requires understanding, compassion, and patience. First-rate cognitive ability is no longer enough for nonprofit executives—these days, they must also have first-rate emotional intelligence.

This is a point that psychologist Daniel Goleman, the author of *Emotional Intelligence: Why It Can Matter More than IQ*, has been making for years. According to Goleman, interpersonal skills are essential to being a successful leader: "My research, along with other recent studies, clearly shows that emotional intelligence is the sine qua non of leadership. Without it, a person can have the best training in the world, an incisive, analytical mind, and an endless supply of great ideas, but he still won't make a great leader."[4]

Goleman points to self-awareness and self-regulation as crucial components of emotional intelligence. These qualities are particularly important in the nonprofit sector. Like all leaders, nonprofit executives must know their limitations so that they can play to their strengths and manage around their weaknesses. But self-understanding is particularly crucial in the nonprofit sector. Many staff members are explicitly seeking "authenticity" in their leaders these days. Of course, it is inappropriate for leaders to be 100% transparent about their thoughts and feelings. But in order to earn trust and motivate their teams, they do need to find a way to speak and act with a degree of candor. It is impossible to do this if you don't understand yourself and cannot keep a firm grip on your emotions.

In an increasingly diverse workplace, empathy is a crucial tool for building rapport across differences of race, class, gender, etc. The bottom line for Goleman is this: "People tend to be very effective at managing relationships when they can understand and control their own emotions and can empathize with the feelings of others."[5]

Flexibility

Harvard's Kennedy School of Government is a place that is obsessed with leadership—it seeks to engage academics and practitioners from a variety of fields in helping to educate the leaders of tomorrow. Even in this environment, Ronald Heifetz stands out. "For decades of students," says former Kennedy School dean Graham T. Allison, "Ron Heifetz is revered as a legend."[6]

Heifetz is famous at Harvard (and beyond) for developing the concept of "adaptive leadership." In concert with several intellectual collaborators, Heifetz has argued that change is inescapable and that no individual, no matter how hard-working or knowledgeable, can hope to have all of the answers to the challenges that confront modern organizations. "The dominant view of leadership is that the leader has the vision and the rest is a sales problem," Heifetz says. "I think that notion of leadership is bankrupt."[7]

Instead, adaptive leaders recognize that experimentation and improvisation are key leadership tools. Writes Heifetz: "Those seeking to lead adaptive change need an experimental mind-set. They must learn to improvise as they go, buying time and resources along the way for the next set of experiments."[8] Another key tool for leaders is reflection. Heifetz and his co-authors encourage leaders to remove themselves from the metaphorical dance floor and "get on the balcony," where they can get a different perspective on what's really happening within their organizations and make adjustments as necessary.

All of this is valuable advice for the modern nonprofit executive. While many nonprofit leaders are monomaniacally focused on achieving a particular goal, the best understand that they need to be flexible about how to reach that goal. The playing field shifts too quickly these days to allow for rigidity of method or dogma of thought. A good steward acknowledges that many new ideas will fail and is willing to pivot when things aren't working.

Humility

Robert K. Greenleaf is the product of another time. Born in 1904, he spent nearly 40 years working at AT&T—the type of stable career that used to be the ideal in America but that no one seems to aspire to anymore. When he retired from the giant communications company, Greenleaf became a consultant, working with the presidents of several universities. This was during the second half of the 1960s, a time when many schools were being torn apart by student unrest over the war in Vietnam and other issues.

Watching the convulsions in higher education, Greenleaf was sympathetic to both students and administrators. He thought that student protest was doing real damage to universities. At the same time, he felt that students had legitimate grievances, including the fact that many professors seemed more focused on their own research than on the art of teaching. According to Greenleaf, "By 1969, I had concluded that the role of teacher at any level calls for a much higher level of dedication to students as their servants than prevailed among faculties at that time."[9]

This insight was the spark that led Greenleaf to develop the concept of "servant leadership." His seminal 1970 essay, "The Servant as Leader," extolled the virtues of humility and power-sharing. According to Greenleaf, the servant leader seeks to ensure that other people's needs are being met rather than focusing on how others can help him to achieve his goals.

This mindset is critical for nonprofit executives. If they are viewed internally as being ego-driven or as using their organizations to glorify themselves, their chances of succeeding are greatly reduced. The idea of servant leadership has a number of implications for how agencies are managed, opening the door to less hierarchical structures and more democratic decision-making.

It also, potentially, has implications for how nonprofit organizations are perceived by the world at large. Yuval Levin's insightful book *A Time to Build* focuses on the problem of declining trust in American institutions. Levin puts his finger on a shifting dynamic within American culture: "We now think of institutions less as formative and more as performative, less as molds of our character and behavior, and more as platforms for us to stand on and be seen. And so . . . we see people using institutions as stages, as a way to raise their profile or build their brand. And those kinds of institutions become much harder to trust."[10]

Too many leaders today view their organizations as platforms or stepping stones. Good stewards are not looking for opportunities to enhance their personal brand. Rather, they think of themselves as servants to the institutions they lead. By adopting a humble, servant mentality, nonprofit executives can not only help build staff morale, they can also help improve public trust in the nonprofit sector.

Long-Term Thinking

Short-term thinking is the default setting for many nonprofit leaders. There are understandable reasons for this. Many organizations are basically living hand-to-mouth. In these settings, nonprofit leaders are justifiably focused on making payroll and surviving to fight another week. Even in places that have a little more of a financial cushion, time horizons can be brief. Some of this is driven by human nature—our attention spans are only so long and few of us are good at planning for the future. And some of this is driven by the impatience and faddishness of foundation and government funders, who tend to want to see a return on their investments as quickly as possible.

Unfortunately, the kinds of problems that nonprofits are trying to tackle—hunger, illness, inequality and the like—tend not to lend themselves to quick victories. And focusing too much on short-term wins can sometimes come with real long-term costs.

This is a lesson that Suzette Brooks Masters learned the hard way.

Masters worked for years in philanthropy, helping to fund organizations engaged in advocacy on behalf of immigrants to America. According to Masters, "I had a single-minded focus on achieving wins for immigrants who faced real suffering and adversity. I felt pressure to identify and fund strategies that could lead to tangible results, such as new policies or sweeping legislation that would improve their lives. I wanted those wins badly, and so did my grantees."[11]

In the aftermath of the presidential election of 2016, where immigration played such a large role in Donald Trump's victory, Masters came to see her work in a new light: "In retrospect, I think my sense of urgency about winning made it more difficult to process dissonant information that didn't align with my strategy. . . . For example, I didn't worry enough about the potential for backlash. I was aware that nativist sentiment was on the rise, and I funded grantees that tracked that rise. But I didn't seek out enough evidence about the unintended negative effects immigration battles could have on a large portion of the public who might have reasonable or principled questions or concerns about demographic changes fueled by immigration."

The dynamic that Masters is describing is not unique to immigration. In many fields, funders and nonprofit agencies have been playing the short game, with perilous consequences to the health of the sector and the country.

Nonprofit leaders must learn to do a delicate dance, meeting the short-term demands of funders while constantly keeping their eyes on the horizon. Morgan Housel, the author of *Same as Ever: A Guide to What Never Changes,* would call this approach "rational optimism." Housel describes rational optimists as "those who acknowledge that history is a constant chain of problems and disappointments and setbacks, but who remain optimistic because they know setbacks don't prevent eventual progress. They sound like hypocrites and flip-floppers, but often they're just looking further ahead than other people."[12]

***

It is all well and good to extol the virtues of emotional intelligence, flexibility, humility, and long-term thinking. I imagine that few nonprofit leaders would dispute the importance of these qualities. But what does good stewardship actually look like in practice? What kinds of activities should nonprofit leaders be engaging in if they hope to guide their organizations through the age of unrest?

There are, of course, a million different ways to embody the values of emotional intelligence, flexibility, humility, and long-term thinking. Every good leader will come up with their own spin. But in talking to my peers and reflecting on what I have seen over the past decade in the sector, I have come to believe that nonprofit leaders must figure out answers to four questions in particular:

Is it possible to expand the number of people involved in meaningful organizational decision-making? While the era of full employment lasts, staffers have more power than they used to—they can always find another job if their current employer isn't to their liking. Plus, as trust in institutions and respect for authority continues to give way, younger staffers are not coming into the workplace in the mood for deference. Given these realities, it is understandable that staffers will want to have a voice in making organizational decisions. How can nonprofits create less hierarchical structures that allow staffers beyond the C-suite to feel like they have had a voice in crafting organization strategy?

How can leaders effectively engage in mentoring across the divides of race, ethnicity, age, sex, gender, and sexuality? The nonprofit workplace is increasingly diverse. The chances that the next generation of leaders within your organization will look just like you is diminishing. It is imperative to the long-term health of nonprofit agencies that younger staffers with leadership potential receive good mentoring. But mentoring young people has become trickier in the age of microaggressions and hostile workplace claims. How can leaders give staffers real mentoring—including honest feedback about the way that they dress or write or present themselves in public—given the realities of the modern-day workplace?

Can mission creep be avoided? The line between successful innovation and debilitating overreach can be perilously thin. In a world with many problems to solve, nonprofits will always be confronted with numerous opportunities to expand into new areas. In recent years, they have also faced the demand that they take positions on issues of public controversy, many of which are outside of their expertise. How can nonprofit leaders maintain organizational discipline and avoid the temptations of mission creep?

When is the right time to step down? This is the ultimate question for every leader. Staying too long at the party is a real and present danger. It is not unusual for nonprofit executive directors to stay in their jobs for 20–30 years. Every situation is unique, of course. Some of these long-serving leaders are doing just fine. But many are over-staying their welcome. There are numerous examples of Baby Boomers doing damage to their organizations by holding on to power for too long. Is it possible for the next generation of leaders to learn from this and engage in thoughtful succession planning?

Each of these questions will be taken up in the chapters ahead.

Chapter 6

Who Decides?

When I first started working in the nonprofit sector in the 1990s, the stereotype of how the typical nonprofit functioned was pretty negative. In many quarters, nonprofits were viewed as flabby, unproductive places where people sat around all day talking about their values rather than going out into the real world to get things done. This was a caricature, of course—there have always been tons of highly productive nonprofit agencies—but it did have a grain of truth to it.

At the time, nonprofit leaders were constantly being entreated to run their organizations like businesses. And many of them tried to do just that. Functionally, this meant a move away from the touchy-feely social justice rhetoric of the 1960s and '70s. It also meant a greater focus on data. Metrics were the mantra of the era. Much of this was driven by philanthropy. It was no longer sufficient to have a handful of good anecdotes or a few heart-wrenching case studies; now foundations wanted to see numbers to document impact.

These kinds of ideas were very much in the air as I cut my teeth as a professional. They definitely helped shape my perspective as I ascended into leadership positions.

When I became the head of the Center for Court Innovation in 2002, I was faced with a number of challenges. Throughout its short life—it was then six years old—the organization had experienced near constant growth. It had recently reached a new plateau: an annual budget of about $11 million and one hundred or so employees.

Many of these employees, and several key external stakeholders, did not express a great deal of confidence when I was named executive director. There were good reasons for this: I was young and untested. Also, I was replacing someone who was widely viewed as a visionary. Many people advised me that the first thing I should do was to organize a strategic planning process that would engage people in the agency with coming up with a new vision for the place.

I ended up ignoring that advice. I didn't want to spend months on what I feared would be a navel-gazing exercise. My instinct was that the organization already had a clear mission and didn't need a new one. People weren't expressing a lack of confidence in our vision—*they were expressing a lack of confidence in* me.

At the same time, I consciously sought to create a more hierarchal organization, with clearer lines of responsibility and decision-making authority. I thought we needed more structure to help deal with our growing size.

Both of these decisions were in some ways anti-democratic, effectively narrowing the circle of those involved in making decisions rather expanding it. You could get away with that kind of thing in 2002, but probably not these days. If someone were to come to me now facing a similar situation and asking for advice, I would never tell them to do what I did. Times have changed, and good leaders need to adapt to this reality.

***

In recent years, public support for organized labor in the United States has increased demonstrably. According to Gallup, in 2022, 71% of Americans said they approved of labor unions, the highest figure recorded since 1965.[1]

While generally we think of unions as being a feature of the public sector or of industry, the newfound American affection for organized labor is also making a dent in the nonprofit sector. It is difficult to find good numbers, but the available evidence suggests that there has been a significant increase in nonprofit union membership. According to the Associated Press, the Nonprofit Professional Employees Union has grown from 300 workers at 12 organizations in 2018 to 1,500 workers at nearly 50 organizations today. And since 2019, the Nonprofit Employees United has unionized workers at 68 organizations.[2] Unions have emerged at a range of prominent nonprofits, including Open Society Foundations, The Marshall Project, and the ACLU as well as many nonprofit museums.

The principal reason why unionization is growing in the nonprofit sector is the same reason why most unions get started: concerns about salary. Many nonprofits pay their employees less than they might make if they worked for government or business. Traditionally, nonprofits have argued that the opportunity to work for a mission-driven organization that offers a better quality of life than can be found in the private or public sector should compensate for reduced pay. But it is understandable that in a good labor market, many employees don't buy this argument and want to advocate for more money.

Unionization appeals to nonprofit workers for reasons beyond compensation. According to John Collier, a union organizer at Community Solutions, a large national nonprofit, "We wanted to have a seat at the table, for the people who were actually doing the work to have a voice."[3]

We have already seen some of the underlying forces driving this desire for greater voice. As outlined in Chapter 3, ideology certainly plays a role—left-wing politics are ascendant in many nonprofits at the moment. And, as Chapter 2 details, the sector has long struggled with the problem of despotic

CEOs ruling their organizations by fiat. Unionization is a logical reaction to this reality.

Advocates for unions argue that they can help improve the culture of nonprofits. According to Alethia Jones, a lecturer in labor studies at City University of New York, "Unions aren't just about the cost point, they can lead to better relationships and more stability."[4]

But many nonprofit leaders think that unionization is a bad fit for the nonprofit sector, the proverbial sledgehammer being used to kill a flea. Nonprofits are typically small, collaborative enterprises where the line between labor and management is blurry. There is no nonprofit equivalent of the factory floor. Does it really make sense to introduce collective bargaining into an organization with a dozen staff people? Won't this inevitably create a more bureaucratic, less innovative, and more adversarial environment?

One nonprofit executive told me, "Unions pit themselves against the organization as a way to organize the employees. This includes fomenting generalized discontent, feeding the flames of trivial grievances, and insulting supervisors and managers (such as insinuating that they don't 'care' about the staff). This ends up changing the dynamic of the organization from one that was a strong team feel to a very divided 'us' vs. 'them' atmosphere."[5]

Unfortunately, very few nonprofit leaders are willing to speak out aggressively against unionization. They understandably fear antagonizing employees and don't want to appear to be "on the wrong side of history." This is probably the wise approach for any given CEO—there is little to be gained from sticking your neck out on this issue. But, taken as a whole, the reticence of nonprofit leaders does a disservice to the field and significantly impoverishes the public debate.

Certainly, it would be catastrophic if the things that nonprofit CEOs whisper behind closed doors turn out to be true—if unionization really does lead to less nimble and effective organizations, the social costs could be enormous. No one wins when nonprofits are expensive, bloated, and slow to respond to emerging challenges. On the other hand, perhaps there will be some unexpected benefits from unionization. It is possible, for example, that unionization might help bolster the bargaining power of nonprofits as they look to negotiate contracts with government.

While unionization is gathering steam in the sector, there are still many more non-unionized nonprofits than there are unionized agencies. What should executives in these organizations be doing? Short of calling for a union, are there ways that these nonprofit leaders can help address concerns about staff voice?

BETWEEN AUTOCRACY AND CHAOS

As I have argued, the days of dictatorial, top-down nonprofit management are coming to an end, if they aren't gone already. And good riddance. For too long, executives labored under the expectation that they were supposed to be nonprofit superheroes—highly charismatic public speakers who simultaneously have a detailed understanding of every nook and cranny of their organization's internal operations. Even the best leader can't be everywhere at once. The myth of the omniscient nonprofit leader has led to a lot of bad practices over the years, including micro-management of staff and unhealthy cult-of-personality work environments.

Vu Lee, a prominent nonprofit blogger and the former executive director of Rainier Valley Corps in Seattle, makes the case for moving beyond a CEO-centric organizational model:

> This decision-making model, which we have unconsciously accepted as the default, is disempowering, inequitable, exhausting, and oftentimes nonsensical. Why should a supervisor, who often only sees a fraction of the frontline work, get to have final say in programmatic matters? Why should I, the [executive director], who spends most of my time outside the office talking to donors and funders . . . get to have ultimate decision-making authority on programs, operations, and other areas that I don't oversee every day? We need a different, better, more rational way of making decisions in our sector.[6]

As Lee makes clear, it is a good thing that many organizations are coming to recognize that too much weight has traditionally been placed on their leaders. On the other hand, if a nonprofit is operating at any kind of scale, it is impossible to run an organization by consensus or by asking for a vote on every decision. Someone needs to be in charge.

The challenge for nonprofit leaders today is to find a middle path between autocracy and organizational chaos. The goal should be to balance the need to give staff meaningful opportunities for input, while maintaining the clear lines of accountability and the ability to move decisively that are the hallmarks of effective organizations.

Some places are attempting to rethink the model of how nonprofits are organized from first principles. The pied piper of this movement is Frederic Laloux, the author of *Reinventing Organizations.* Laloux, a Belgian social entrepreneur who spent time as a management consultant at McKinsey & Company, is an advocate of self-management, arguing for organizations without hierarchies or bosses. Just as "there is no single tree in charge of the whole forest," Laloux believes that organizational decision-making should not be in the hands of a single CEO, but rather spread out to the entire team:[7]

> The world is getting more and more complex, to a point where the complexity indeed exceeds what any leader, however bright and hard-working, can deal with. So we need to shift to processes of collective intelligence. But to do that, we will need to create entirely different organizational structures and processes, because the good old pyramid, with its rigid reporting lines that converge at the top, is incompatible with—and hostile to—processes of collective intelligence. The tradition[al] approach forces people to decide from one single functional perspective, in a top-down fashion.[8]

Laloux's vision of collective intelligence has inspired hundreds of organizations to question the standard approach to doing business—rethinking the C-suite, job descriptions, budgets, target goals, and much more. While Laloux's ideas seem to have gained more traction in the business world than the nonprofit sector, there are a handful of nonprofits that are working to reimagine the traditional nonprofit structure by dramatically flattening hierarchies. The goal, as Nicole Wales of the Nonprofit Democracy Network articulates it, is to create "liberatory structures" where "power can be shared rather than hoarded, a culture of care and reciprocity can replace one of exploitation and overwork, [and] conflict can be generative and restorative rather than divisive and toxic."[9]

One example is the "worker self-directed nonprofit" model, exemplified by the Sustainable Economies Law Center in Oakland, California. To engage staff in making organizational decisions, the Law Center has created a series of staff "circles" with well-delineated zones of authority.

Perhaps predictably, the organizations that are attracted to this kind of working arrangement tend to be small and hyper-progressive. Some of them have struggled to stay afloat financially.[10] Even the most committed advocates of the self-directed model admit that it takes a lot of time to transition to this new way of thinking. Another problem is the reality that old habits die hard. Even in the absence of a formal hierarchy, great care must be employed to prevent an informal elite from emerging to dominate decision-making.[11]

If Laloux and self-directed management are at the woo-woo, revolutionary end of the spectrum, participatory budgeting is more of a reformist idea.

Participatory budgeting grows out of the insight that "budgets are moral documents." Looking at how an organization spends its money has always been a good way to determine what its priorities are. That's why nonprofit CEOs tend to exercise tight control over their organizational budgets. Not only are staff generally not included in the budgeting process, but in many places the budget is not shared with staff even after it has been formalized and approved by the board. The organization's finances are effectively a black box, creating an enormous information asymmetry between those who know what's in the budget and those who don't.

Participatory budgeting seeks to change this dynamic, giving staff a say in how an organization's budget is allocated. The idea first emerged as an experiment in direct democracy in Brazil in 1989. Since then, it has spread to thousands of cities around the world.[12] Participatory budgeting looks different from place to place, but typically a certain amount of a jurisdiction's budget is set aside to be determined by the public through direct engagement. A formal process is articulated, and local residents are then given an opportunity both to submit ideas for how the money should be spent and to vote on what should get funded.

Participatory budgeting has begun to migrate from the public sector to the nonprofit sector. For example, in 2022, inspired by participatory budgeting, CompassPoint, a leadership development organization in California, decided to have staff participate in creating their annual budget. According to finance director Monica Marie Avery, the goal was to create a process that would intentionally challenge "the assumption that a small executive and/or financial team holds all the answers and hands down a budget to the rest of the organization."[13] CompassPoint appointed "budget managers" across the organization who were responsible for soliciting input from staff. In addition, they facilitated a series of learning sessions designed to help teach staff the rudiments of finance, so that they had the knowledge and vocabulary necessary to offer informed opinions.

Another initiative that contains elements of participatory budgeting is taking place at the Center for Justice Innovation (my old shop). The Center has created a special $1 million innovation fund in their annual budget. Staff are asked to propose projects that would test new ideas or address unmet needs. A committee comprised of both staff and external experts weighs the proposals and awards grants to a handful of winners. In addition to the money, the Center has also committed to using its time and connections to help move the winning ideas to implementation. "It's a concrete way for us to give staff at all levels of the organization a role in dreaming up what comes next for us," says executive director Courtney Bryan.

Self-directed organizations and iterations on participatory budgeting are just two of many different approaches that nonprofit leaders can explore to strengthen the voice of staff in their operations. Other examples include surveys, town halls, staff advisory councils, 360-degree performance reviews that allow employees to offer feedback about supervisors, and open office hours where staff at all levels of the hierarchy can get face time with the executive director without an appointment. There is no one-size-fits-all solution, of course. What works in a small, community-based start-up is unlikely to make sense in a national organization, and vice versa.

CAVEAT EMPTOR

While giving staff a greater voice is a worthy goal, nonprofit executives should proceed with eyes wide open—there are many potential pitfalls to democratizing decision-making within an organization.

- *Fake Engagement*: Staff are pretty good at sensing when a process is just for show, with no real impact on decision-making. In an era of profound skepticism about authority, nonprofit leaders will want to avoid the accusation that they are engaged in an exercise in "window dressing." Leaders need to be genuinely open to input from staff—even if they disagree with what they hear or if staff sometimes advance legitimately bad ideas.
- *Unrealistic Expectations*: At the other end of the spectrum, nonprofit executives need to be wary of creating a set of expectations that they cannot meet. Bold declarations about staff democracy can create the impression that staff are being given significant decision-making authority.

Leaders should take pains to communicate clearly what is fair game and what is not. In general, it is wise to follow the old business dictum: under-promise and over-deliver. Failure to do so runs the risk of engendering disillusionment and deepening cynicism. Staff should understand that their input is valued, but that it is impossible to implement every suggestion they make.

- *Time Is of the Essence*: One of the most common complaints about organizational life is an excess of meetings. Creating new vehicles for staff engagement almost inevitably means adding additional meetings to an already-crowded calendar. Because (most) people hate meetings, nonprofit executives should be parsimonious as they look to democratize decision-making. Creating more meetings and adding responsibilities to the plate of overworked employees is one way to succeed in creating a more democratic institution but fail to increase staff satisfaction. It can also lead to the dreaded "paralysis by analysis," as issues are deliberated endlessly without driving to a decision.
- *Too Much Intention*: Nonprofit leaders are constantly being hectored these days to be more "transparent" and "intentional." It is hard to argue against transparency and thoughtfulness, but like anything else, these values can sometimes be taken too far. Designing explicit rules and guidelines and processes for everything under the sun can take some of the joy and mystery out of organizational life. It is ok to keep some things loose, to create room for improvisation, informality, and serendipity.

But the biggest cautionary note for nonprofit leaders who are interested in decentralizing authority is that they need to listen to both the words and the music when soliciting staff input.

There is a reason why, not that long ago, bosses would adorn their desks with the message "the buck stops here." While lots of people talk about wanting to have a role in making decisions, the truth is that, when push comes to shove, many do not actually want the pressure and responsibility that accompanies making the really hard calls. Many people are, in fact, happy to pass the buck.

Which programs will get axed when a budget shortfall emerges? Should the organization accept a big new grant from a government funder even though that funder's inability to pay on time will put enormous pressure on the organization's ability to meet payroll? Which of two internal candidates should get the big promotion? How should a conflict between important staffers be adjudicated? Does a well-liked employee's chronic underperformance merit termination? Dozens of questions like these must be resolved every year in the life of a typical nonprofit organization. It is very difficult to imagine these decisions being subject to a group decision-making process involving dozens of people. Sometimes, unpopular decisions need to be made for the greater good of an organization and its mission.

The traditional command-and-control version of nonprofit leadership is, thankfully, being rethought by many organizations. But even as this happens, it is worth remembering why the pyramid structure, with a powerful CEO at the top, emerged in the first place. Someone has to make the tough decisions. Someone has to be accountable for the success or failure of an agency. If everyone is responsible, then no one is.

Chapter 7

The Nonprofit Mentoring Crisis

When I was the head of the Center for Court Innovation, young people would frequently come into my office and tell me that they were looking for a mentor. I often felt at a loss for how to guide them. It has always been my strong suspicion that it is difficult to engineer a mentoring relationship—ideally it is something that happens organically rather than as a result of some sort of formal strategy.

But I rarely said that. Instead, what I tended to do was push them to articulate why they felt like they needed a mentor and what they expected a mentor to do for them. What I often heard back was not so much a desire for a mentor but a wish for a fairy godmother—someone endlessly benevolent and all powerful who would be capable of removing professional obstacles whenever they appeared.

Maybe that kind of mentoring exists, but I've never seen it. Instead, what I have seen—and participated in, both as mentor and mentee—are what I would describe as relationships of mutual benefit. I don't mean this to sound crass or Machiavellian. In my professional travels, I have met plenty of people that I liked and that I wished the best for. But only a handful have developed into meaningful mentoring relationships. Invariably, these were with people who I thought could help the Center for Court Innovation advance in significant ways. Self-interest always plays a role at some level.

As I prodded the visitors to my office to adopt more realistic expectations, I would encourage them to think about the people they knew who were ahead of them on the professional ladder. Who did they respect? Who had they learned from? Instead of looking for the one true mentor who would selflessly serve them for the rest of their lives, I urged young people to recognize that they already had mentors in their lives and that they could cobble together a handful to meet different kinds of needs.

The most important professional mentor I have ever had was John Feinblatt, my predecessor as the executive director of the Center for Court Innovation. I first met John when I moved to New York City in 1992. I have had a chance to work with hundreds of people since then, including famous academics, high-ranking government officials, powerful foundation executives, and more. John remains the most impressive professional that I have ever encountered. Smart, strategic, and driven, he is the rare person capable of both articulating big-picture vision and thinking through the gritty details of implementation.

John played a crucial role in my career, helping to promote me, both literally and figuratively. But John wasn't always kind. In fact, sometimes he could be quite tough, judging my work harshly and demanding more time and effort from me. If you had asked me to draw up my ideal mentor from scratch, I almost certainly would have described someone who was more obviously nurturing. And on many issues, John and I didn't see eye-to-eye. Still, John had one major advantage over the mentor of my dreams: he had the benefit of actually existing in real life.

I would imagine that John would say that I was an imperfect mentee in all sorts of ways. But I think he would also say that I helped him to achieve things that he might not have accomplished without my assistance. Or at least I hope he would say that because, in my experience, the best relationships, including mentoring relationships, are based on reciprocity.

These days, if people ask me, I tell them not to look for mentors but to search instead for people that they admire who need their help. The recipe for finding a mentor is simple: make yourself useful.

***

Eboo Patel has been in and around the nonprofit sector for quite some time. More than twenty years ago he founded a nonprofit that has grown into a national organization called Interfaith America that works to promote religious diversity and interfaith cooperation, particularly on college campuses. As a sideline, Patel also serves as a columnist for *The Chronicle of Philanthropy*, where he has been an astute observer of the unrest that has roiled so many organizations in recent years.

Taking stock of the playing field in early 2024, Patel made the case that one of the casualties of nonprofit tumult has been the quality of the relationships between senior and junior staffers. In a piece titled "A Nonprofit Mentoring Crisis Threatens Future Leadership of the Field," Patel argues that many nonprofit executives have effectively ceased giving meaningful feedback to their employees for fear of engendering complaints or litigation. He writes:

> My greatest moments of learning occurred when someone who was my senior took me aside and told me what I was doing wrong . . . . My life is full of countless such incidents—each essential to my growth as a leader, and all of them supremely uncomfortable when they occurred. I fear my kids, ages 13 and 16, will not have such life-changing opportunities, particularly if they go into social-sector work. Why? Well, let me put it this way. Do *you* give unvarnished advice to students or interns or junior staff the way you might have 10 or 20 years ago—the

> way your mentors gave you advice? Why would you if providing even standard feedback to an employee might lead to a grievance claim that triggers a human-resources investigation? Why risk offering guidance if you could be publicly branded as a racist and a sexist for advice as pedestrian as how to dress professionally?[1]

A 2022 survey found that nearly one out of three employers reported an increase in employee grievances. Relationships with managers were one of the primary sources of conflict.[2]

Some of this activity is no doubt a good thing—employees should complain if they have been the subject of harassing or abusive behavior. But something seems to have shifted in the underlying dynamics of our country.

AN AGE OF GRIEVANCE

New York Times columnist Frank Bruni has argued that we are living through an "age of grievance." According to Bruni, too many Americans are asking, "How have I been wronged? Who wronged me? What am I owed? And how do I get back at them? And it is such a negative and corrosive approach that takes just causes and mingles them with petty complaints. Or that takes just causes and blows them so wildly out of proportion that they no longer seem warranted."[3]

This is a society-wide problem, of course, but it has particularly negative implications for nonprofit organizations. How can nonprofit executives create meaningful bonds with junior staffers if they are constantly looking over their shoulders, worried about potential HR complaints or union grievances? And how can the next generation of talent receive the real-world advice and coaching they need in order to mature into leadership if nonprofit executives are treating them with kid gloves?

It's not like nonprofits were doing a bang-up job of developing talent in the years before the great unrest. A national survey of nearly 6,000 non-executive staffers conducted in 2008 documented a host of concerns with nonprofit leadership development, including "lack of support and mentorship from incumbent executives."[4]

Organizations with the wherewithal to do so would be well served to invest in deliberate programming designed to develop emerging leaders, including linking them to mentors both internally and externally. But the reality is that many, if not most, nonprofits simply do not have the kinds of resources required to create formal leadership development programs. In these places, mentoring tends to be done on an ad hoc basis.

Perhaps that's for the best in some respects. Good mentoring relationships depend upon two people establishing a level of comfort and trust with one another. That's often easier to do when a relationship develops spontaneously rather than through some sort of formal matchmaking process.

The problem with relying on ad hoc mentoring is that this means it often doesn't happen. For the typical nonprofit executive, there are always more urgent problems to attend to than nurturing in-house talent.

That's a shame, because nonprofit leaders tend to say that mentoring has been important to their careers. Nonprofit mentoring is particularly important because of the diversity and idiosyncrasy of the sector—nonprofits can differ wildly from one to another. You can get a graduate degree in nonprofit management, but that will only teach you a limited amount about what it means to actually run a specific institution. For that, the best teacher, other than experience, is to hear it from the horse's mouth—the men and women who have done the job in real life.

Joan Garry is a consultant who has coached numerous nonprofit executives over the years. Her practice grows out of her experience as the executive director of GLAAD, one of the most prominent LGBTQ organizations in the country. According to Garry,

> When I first arrived at GLAAD, I knew that I needed some real support if I was going to successfully transition from the for-profit sector. This new nonprofit world I had entered was strange! What I really needed was a navigator, a guide for coaching for executives, someone to help me learn the ropes and provide some wisdom about what it meant to be a leader in a movement. But you can't always get what you want . . . or need . . . . But I got very lucky. The choice just happened. A colleague [executive director] with a long nonprofit history extended herself because she saw my success as important to the movement . . . . I took her up on it. Turned out to be one of the smartest moves I made. Thanks to her, I learned the ropes and avoided falling on my face a few times.[5]

Garry's testimony resonates with the experience of a great many nonprofit executives. "Mentorship is essential for any positive change," argues Amy Ellenbogen, who served as the director of Neighbors in Action, a community safety program in central Brooklyn for 17 years. "Good mentors have helped me notice 'what I don't yet know I don't know' and expanded the bubble of ideas within which I operate."

Mentoring almost always requires the bridging of difference—most mentors are older than their mentees, so both sides need to figure out how to overcome an age gap in order to connect with one another. In addition to the generational divide, mentoring these days often involves bridging differences of class, race, ethnicity, sexuality, religion, and gender, among other divides.

How can leaders forge effective mentoring relationships with subordinates in an age of nonprofit unrest? Three things are critical.

Trust

Trust is the lubricant that greases the nonprofit machine. Perhaps because trust is such a precious commodity, many nonprofit leaders take a "wait-and-see" approach with their teams, essentially demanding that staff prove that they are worthy of trust through their performance and loyalty. While this is understandable on many levels, it can be an impediment to effective mentoring.

In general, nonprofit leaders should make the first move—giving trust in order to engender trust in turn. Demonstrating trust is particularly important given the cynicism about institutions that many young employees bring with them to the workplace.

Make no mistake: trusting staffers to do the right thing and perform at a high level without undue scrutiny or excessive accountability measures is a risk. Some will inevitably disappoint. But most will not.

In my experience, the advantages of showing trust far outweigh the costs. Taking this leap of faith, giving staff members room to operate and make decisions without constantly looking over their shoulders, will inure to a leader's benefit in the long run. Giving trust is a valuable management tool that will help nonprofit executives develop the kind of internal credibility that they will inevitably need when it comes time to make and communicate hard decisions about where the organization is going, what projects will get prioritized, and who will be promoted. It is also important to good mentoring—within the relationship, mentees must feel like they are interacting with a real person and getting access to information that is authentic and valuable.

Reciprocity

The best relationships are two-way streets. This kernel of folk wisdom has also made its way into the academic literature, thanks in no small part to Edwin P. Hollander. Hollander, who died in 2020, was a professor of psychology who wrote frequently about organizational leadership. In particular, Hollander was obsessed with the relationship between leaders and followers. How is power won? What gives leaders legitimacy? How do they build up enough credit with supporters to generate compliance, and even enthusiasm, when they want to move a group in a new direction?

In answering these questions, Hollander sought to advance an inclusive brand of leadership that focused the energies of leaders on doing things *with* people rather than *to* people. Hollander thought the role of followers had gotten short shrift from academic theorists. While there were hundreds of books devoted to the traits and strategies of effective leaders, very few professors were writing about what it meant to be a good follower. This struck Hollander as a massive gap in the literature—after all, it was impossible to be a leader without followers.

According to Hollander, relations between leaders and followers are transactions in which the follower plays an active role.

No one has to be a follower, of course—at any given moment, followers can effectively accept or reject their leaders. But Hollander went further, arguing that followers exert influence over leaders. Indeed, Hollander believed that a leader's influence over followers is purchased at the price of allowing the followers to influence him or her in turn. To Hollander, the leader–follower relationship rests on a foundation of mutual influence.[6]

The same holds true for mentoring relationships. The best, most influential and long-lasting pairings inevitably involve some form of give-and-take. Mentors want to see their proteges absorbing and enacting whatever wisdom they have chosen to impart. Proteges might not have the same expectations in reverse, but effective leaders should stay alert to what they can learn from their proteges.

"The people you mentor may be junior to you professionally, but they often have skills and insights you don't have," says Amy Barasch, who served for a decade as the leader of Her Justice, an organization that provides free legal services to women living in poverty in New York. "They can also serve as a reality check, letting you know if the messages you are sending don't make sense or aren't landing with staff." In my experience, I have found that making small changes in language, gesture, or orientation can have powerful symbolic value, signaling to a mentee that they are valued and that their voice matters.

Generosity

I have already extolled the virtues of servant leadership at length, so I won't do it again here, but suffice to say that good mentoring is an example of servant leadership in action. Bill Gates has said that "There are two great forces of human nature—self-interest and caring for others."[7] To be effective mentors, nonprofit executives have to lean into the latter.

When you lead an organization, you are a magnet for information. You have access to every department within your agency. You understand the finances. You know the proposals that are being submitted to fund future projects. You have a catbird seat that provides you with a unique perspective on organizational dynamics.

But that's not all. You also are the first point of entry for many external actors who want to engage with your organization, whether they be reporters or government officials or potential partners. These kinds of interactions tend to bring with them news and gossip from the outside world—Who is thinking about running for office? Who just accepted a new job? What were they saying at the big national conference? As a result, the best nonprofit executive directors tend to develop a strong sense of the fields in which they work.

To do right by their mentees, executives must be charitable with some (but by no means all) of this information. There's no doubt that nonprofit executives often have to be self-protecting. It is not always possible to explain to a mentee exactly why a specific decision has been made. There are some obvious bright lines to observe around personnel and HR issues, but there are also lots of gray areas. Figuring out how to navigate them prudently is an important part of being a good nonprofit mentor. The goal should be to present mentees with a window into the real-life pressures and trade-offs that come with the job, rather than a sanitized version of executive life.

Opening up your rolodex is another important part of being a generous mentor. Amy Ellenbogen, the former director of Neighbors in Action, makes that clear: "Mentors have shown up for me by making time in their calendars for thought partnership and sharing their networks with me with a generous spirit," she says. "Some mentors have created a 'place at the table' for me by inviting me to events for which I was not originally on the guest list, offering me opportunities to speak, and publicly and privately acknowledging my contributions."

Finally, perhaps the most important—and most uncomfortable—part of generosity is providing honest feedback. As Eboo Patel of Interfaith America argues, it can be incredibly valuable when someone who is senior to you explains what you are doing wrong.

I have definitely benefited from this kind of tough love in my career. At various points, I have been told to change the way I dress, to tweak my public speaking style, and to spend more hours in the office, among other constructive criticisms. While sometimes painful, this feedback was delivered in a generous spirit, with a goal of improving my performance. I was fortunate to receive it.

***

There are no easy solutions to the problem of nonprofit unrest. Creating nurturing, mentoring relationships with employees will not, by itself, lead to harmonious and effective nonprofit organizations. But it can be a valuable piece in the puzzle, helping to humanize chief executives and offering concrete evidence that they care about more than their own advancement. At a time when trust in nonprofit institutions is flagging, this kind of effort is all the more important.

As we have seen in Chapter 4, mentoring is also an important tool in the fight to increase diversity in nonprofit leadership. Getting in the door is only half the battle for people of color and members of other marginalized groups. Rising through the ranks is a different kind of challenge. Believing it is possible is an essential part of the process.

A mentoring relationship can help young people debunk common myths about nonprofit leadership. It can show them that you don't have to be a genius or work 24 hours a day in order to run a nonprofit. Access to the brains and the networks of current leaders can serve as rocket fuel for an aspiring nonprofit staffer, helping them to broaden their horizons, set ambitious goals, and reach their potential.

Yuval Levin of the American Enterprise Institute has devoted a good chunk of his career to thinking about leadership and the challenge of how to build legitimacy. "We trust an institution when it seems to have an ethic that makes the people within it more trustworthy," Levin argues. "However, we lose faith in an institution when we no longer believe that it plays that kind of ethical or formative role shaping the people within it to be trustworthy."

The challenge for nonprofit leaders is to demonstrate, both internally and externally, that they are trustworthy. Being a good mentor to aspiring young people is one way to do that. "'Given my role here, how should I behave?'—That's what somebody who takes an institution seriously would ask," says Levin. "A lot of the trouble that's facing our core institutions now might be described as a widespread failure to ask that kind of question."[8]

Nonprofit leaders are not the only ones who should be asking themselves the question "Given my role here, how should I behave?" If junior staffers at nonprofit organizations reflect on the same question, they might decide to strive to be good mentees. Effective mentoring is driven by the mentee as much as by the mentor. Being open to advice and constructive feedback is not easy, particularly in a time when there are so many voices suggesting that leaders are not to be trusted. But it is essential to a good mentoring relationship.

"Having a mentor can absolutely be a powerful asset for your personal and professional growth," leadership coach Mark Nevins writes. "However, if you are not able or willing to put in the work it takes to invest in the relationship and apply the knowledge you gain, then a mentor cannot help you, regardless of how successful they personally have been."[9]

Music producer Phil Ramone, who was responsible for hits by Billy Joel, Paul Simon, and numerous other artists, made the case most succinctly: "You can only mentor somebody if *they* want to be mentored."[10]

Chapter 8

Mission Creep

When I was the head of the Center for Court Innovation, I was often asked about our organization's mission statement. That's because for years, we didn't have one. This flummoxed some of our funders—and not a few staffers as well.

I had a few different answers for why I was resistant to the idea of a mission statement. The first was that the Center for Court Innovation didn't need a mission statement because the name of our organization was, in effect, a mission statement.

If that didn't work, I would argue that mission statements, as printed on a page, were mostly useless. If funders or staffers wanted to know what the organization was all about, I thought they should come look at our work, not some abstract words. This was my way of saying that performed values are always more important than stated values.

I also didn't want a mission statement because I didn't want the organization to be boxed in. Because we had "innovation" in our name, I thought we should have the widest possible latitude to try new things and test new ideas.

I would also admit that I could be a bit of a contrarian. I liked the idea of defying the conventional wisdom, which said that every nonprofit needed a mission statement.

I could hold out for only so long, however. As the organization got bigger, it became harder and harder to resist the calls for a mission statement. I couldn't count on newcomers intuitively understanding what the agency was about.

Eventually, I caved to the inevitable, authorizing not only a mission statement but a tag line as well. The fact that I cannot recall the precise language of either today is probably a sign that, in my heart of hearts, I never really committed myself to the idea of a mission statement.

With the benefit of hindsight, however, I think I was probably in the wrong all along. Watching many nonprofits struggle to maintain organizational discipline in recent years has led me to believe that narrower, more precise mission statements are, in the main, probably better for nonprofits than broader ones.

***

Nonprofit mission statements tend to be dull, earnest affairs.

They are often written by committee. And you can usually tell. There is an epic-list quality to many mission statements, as organizations try every trick in the book, including multiple parenthetical statements, to stuff as many ideas as possible into the minimum number of sentences.

Another regular feature of mission statements is the use of imprecise language. Mission statements are full of calls to "promote justice," "strengthen communities," "create opportunity," and the like. Who could be against such goals? How these vague concepts translate into action in the real world is anyone's guess.

So the average nonprofit mission statement is hardly a work of art. More clunky than artistic, more hazy than precise, mission statements rarely tell you very much about what organizations are really up to.

But still.

For all of their flaws, mission statements do offer some basic guardrails for nonprofits, defining a scope of work, however broad. And the past few years have offered ample evidence of how tempting it can be for nonprofits to ignore those guardrails.

A few examples, among many:

Similar to Bronx Defenders, which we saw in Chapter 3 embroiled in a controversy over the war in Gaza, Planned Parenthood, an organization focused on reproductive rights and health, also issued a statement on Israel. Unlike Bronx Defenders, Planned Parenthood tried not to take sides. Perhaps as a result, the statement somehow managed to please approximately 0% of the people who read it, including the organization's own employees who denounced it as "disinformation."[1]

The Wende Museum, a museum in Culver City, California, dedicated to preserving Cold War material culture, announced its plans to build housing for the homeless.[2]

The Sunrise Movement, an environmental group, decided it was within their remit to host online trainings about defunding the police.[3]

Why are these nonprofits, and others like them, engaged in work that, at least to the outside observer, feels so far beyond their ken?

There are good and bad reasons.

THE DISEASE OF MORE

There is a great deal of truth to the old saying that organizations are like sharks: if they stop moving forward, they die. Yesterday's innovation is tomorrow's conventional wisdom that needs to be overturned. Healthy organizations adapt to changing conditions and problems as they emerge.

Pat Riley, back when he was the coach of the Los Angeles Lakers in the 1980s, had a talented team that he thought was capable of winning the NBA title year after year. One of the most formidable impediments to the dynasty that Riley envisioned was what he called the "disease of more." According to Riley, after a team won a championship, everyone wanted more. Stars wanted more money. Supporting talent wanted more credit. Bench players wanted more shots. All of these demands were a constant threat to the fragile chemistry that had enabled team success in the first place.

Riley is not the only person to suggest that success contains the seeds of failure, of course. And the disease of more applies to venues other than professional sports. We see traces of it when celebrity actors decide they want to be directors. Or when Bob Dylan declares that he wants to be a painter. Or when businessmen conclude that they have the answers to our political problems. Put simply, successful people find it hard to stay in their lanes.

The nonprofit sector is hardly immune to the disease of more. Those who are responsible for a successful initiative often find themselves asked to scale it up or to do it again in other places. The temptation to say yes to these entreaties is enormous. Lord knows I have participated in plenty of brainstorming sessions where the task at hand was to come up with new potential applications of strategies that had proven successful in the past in other settings.

The need for constant reinvention in the nonprofit sector is driven by many forces. Sometimes it is a byproduct of success. And sometimes it is a byproduct of the whims of philanthropy, which can often be faddish and impatient. Foundations have often favored short funding cycles (typically three years) and project funding over general operating support. Both of these predispositions incentivize nonprofits to manufacture new programs and new initiatives so that they can successfully market themselves to foundations.

Another factor that encourages nonprofits to look beyond their usual remit is a simple one: there are plenty of problems to solve in the world. The daily fodder of nonprofit life is failure and tragedy. Every day, nonprofit workers encounter government systems that don't work as well as they should and hard luck stories where, through no fault of their own, people find themselves living in dire conditions and dealing with desperate situations. It is understandable that many nonprofits, when confronted with these realities, feel compelled to try to jump into the breach.

All of these dynamics have been at work in the nonprofit sector for years now. What feels different these days is the pressure on many organizations to embrace a broad range of progressive causes. Thus, the assertions that "climate justice is racial justice," or that the war in Gaza is somehow central to the fight for reproductive freedom. Universities are asked to pursue social justice, not just the production of knowledge or the education of students. It is no longer enough for direct service organizations to aid the needy; they must also engage in advocacy to change the systems that oppress them.

For left-wing activists, the argument driving these developments is simple: the world is full of injustice and it's up to all of us to do our part to address the injustice we see. Elizabeth Merritt, the director of the Center for the Future of Museums, argues that "mission creep" is just another way of saying "going out of our way to do the right thing." According to Merritt,

> Perhaps in a more functional world it would be enough for a museum to focus just on being great at preserving and interpreting art, or science, or history. If, for example, we had

> systems that equitably addressed everyone's basic needs and fundamental rights. But we don't. We live in a patchwork of imperfect solutions that leave many needs unmet and many people deprived of rights. . . . Museums are integral parts of our social and economic systems. They can use their power and authority to reinforce the status quo (if only through inaction), or they can do their part to improve these systems where they fall short.[4]

Nonprofit blogger Vu Le believes we need to rethink the idea that mission creep is a bad thing. "Organizations led by marginalized communities often have broad missions," Le argues. "This broadness is often seen as a weakness, a lack of organization, when in reality it is a culturally-relevant necessity."[5] For Le, a tight organizational focus is a luxury that many agencies led by people of color cannot afford.

LIKE KUDZU

There are legitimate arguments to be made on behalf of a nonprofit extending its reach, but mission creep can be an insidious opponent, weaponizing an organization's instinct for compassion and innovation against itself. Dolph Goldenburg, host of the Successful Nonprofits podcast, has likened mission creep to kudzu: "A hundred plus years ago, we brought kudzu to the United States thinking, 'Oh, this is going to be great. It's going to make great feed for our cows and our goats and everything else that we like to get milk from and eat.' And then it turns out that it was an invasive species and took over most of the southeastern United States. That's sort of what mission creep looks like."[6]

Consultants Kim Jonker and William F. Meehan, writing in the *Stanford Social Innovation Review,* argue that nonprofits must constantly be on alert if they hope to combat mission creep:

> Mission creep plagues the nonprofit sector. In the private sector, pencil manufacturers, for example, rarely dive into the bakery business or into human resources consulting. Yet nonprofits routinely do the equivalent, expanding their programs far beyond their organizations' original scope, skills, and core competencies—often in response to funding opportunities or staff members' interests. This creeping can stretch organizations so thin and so far that they can no longer effectively apply their resources toward their goals.[7]

The problem of mission creep is both obvious and subtle. As Jonker and Meehan indicate, nonprofits, if they are any good, develop a set of core competencies over time. When they depart from their area of expertise—say, when a museum decides to become a developer of affordable housing—nonprofits face considerable risk. First, they face the risk of failure and then they face the risk of reputational damage. As Warren Buffet has suggested, a reputation takes years to build, but it can be ruined in mere minutes. Once a nonprofit has tarnished its reputation with a foolhardy initiative or an ill-considered statement, it may struggle for years to restore its good name.

Mission creep poses a particular threat to advocacy organizations. Jeremiah Johnson of the Center for New Liberalism has argued that these organizations are dealing with a metastasizing case of social justice—"if you are an activist for one cause, you're expected to speak up about all causes now."[8] One effect of this is that single-issue organizations now face enormous pressure to comment on issues outside of their narrow focus.

This seemingly innocuous dynamic comes with enormous costs. When a climate change organization also takes stands on issues like Israel or policing or trans identity, it effectively signals that it is a progressive organization. In the process, it significantly narrows the appeal of its primary message.

There are plenty of people across the political spectrum who might be convinced to endorse new approaches to climate change. But how many will also want to sign on to the organization's position on a range of other controversial issues? The number shrinks dramatically with each new position an organization takes. "The ultimate result of activist mission creep," as Jeremiah Johnson illustrates, "is that your issue ceases to be something that people across the ideological spectrum can work together on. It becomes coded as a red tribe vs. blue tribe issue, gets swallowed by the general culture war, and progress grinds to a halt as partisan warfare starts."

There is some evidence to suggest that this phenomenon actually undermines organizational effectiveness. In a study of the historical impact of interest groups on American policy outcomes, political scientist Matt Grossmann finds that liberal advocacy groups like the ACLU and the Sierra Club have traditionally performed "way above their organizational weight" in part because of their ability to partner in broad coalitions. According to Grossmann, these groups have "benefited from strong single-issue reputations that differentiated them from the generic image of the left."[9] In other words, when contemporary nonprofits move away from a narrow organizational focus and tie themselves to "the generic image of the left," they are likely to undermine their ability to influence policy.

So how can nonprofit leaders avoid the dangers of mission drift?

A good first step would be to take another look at their organization's mission statement. Chances are good that it needs some tightening up. Mission statements shouldn't be a straitjacket, an impossible-to-break cellphone contract that ties nonprofits down unnecessarily. Nonprofits will always need some wiggle room so that they can easily respond to new challenges without always having to go back to first principles. Still, there have to be limits. A good mission statement functions in much the same way as the U.S. Constitution does—it serves as a touchstone that can guide an organization through troubled waters and help it figure out when to say yes and when to say no to new opportunities.

According to Kim Jonker and William F. Meehan, a well-honed mission statement has seven characteristics: "It is focused. It solves unmet public needs. It leverages unique skills. It guides trade-offs. It inspires, and is inspired by, key stakeholders. It anticipates change. And it sticks in memory."[10]

Unfortunately, as Jonker and Meehan observe, very, very few nonprofit mission statements meet these standards. Far more common are overly broad statements of purpose that encompass a dizzying array of activities. Nonprofits might find that saying they are doing less could actually help them accomplish more. A narrowly focused mission statement can be a valuable tool in the effort to explain to importuning staffers and funders why an organization cannot take on tasks that are a distraction from core activities.

Nonprofits would also be well-advised to think about whether it is necessary for them to take positions on political issues outside of their area of expertise. In recent months, a number of educational institutions have backed away from issuing such statements, choosing to embrace the principles of institutional neutrality articulated in the University of Chicago's 1967 Kalven Report. Disagreement over the war in Gaza has been the driving force behind this development; schools realized that they would not be able to come up with a position that simultaneously satisfied both their pro-Palestine and pro-Israel constituents, so they used the conflict as an opportunity to get out of the business of making statements altogether.

In general, this is a healthy development—universities and other educational institutions have done a lot of damage to their reputations by unnecessarily speaking out on issues of controversy. Most nonprofits would do well to follow their lead.

Nonprofits are, of course, susceptible to the same kinds of pressure that rocked so many universities in 2023–24: major donors deciding that they were unhappy with a political statement (or lack thereof) and deciding to withdraw their support from offending institutions. By not commenting on the issues of the day, nonprofits can avoid becoming a target of angry donors. This would also put nonprofits in a stronger position to protect their staff and clients if they choose to exercise their rights to engage in unpopular political commentary or activism.

Finally, nonprofits should be taking a hard look in the mirror every few years. Is there still a need for what we do? Are we still relevant? Have we largely succeeded in fulfilling our core goals? These are the kind of fundamental questions that nonprofits should be asking themselves every half decade or so.

One of the most corrosive arguments that critics levy against nonprofits is that they are more interested in self-perpetuation than they are in solving social problems. I don't believe this is true.

Nevertheless, nonprofits should still take this line of attack seriously. They can no longer count on people giving them the benefit of the doubt just because they have good intentions—they must take pains to demonstrate that they are not self-interested actors.

One way nonprofits can do that is by rigorously assessing their programs on a regular basis—and demonstrating their willingness to shut down programs when they have outlived their usefulness. I know from first-hand experience how hard this can be. Indeed, my instincts when I was the director of a large nonprofit pointed in the other direction—I almost always sought to keep projects alive, sometimes in the face of significant obstacles.

But the truth is that the United States probably has more than enough nonprofits. Culling the redundant, the irrelevant, and the ineffective would be in society's best interests.

When asked, many nonprofit leaders are prone to say that their ultimate goal is to put themselves out of business. That is, they hope to be so successful at whatever their mission is—curing cancer, housing the homeless, mastering malnutrition, etcetera—that their organization would be rendered superfluous.

Of course, this almost never happens. Success is elusive on many fronts. And many nonprofits have missions that are truly evergreen: there will always be a need to tend to the sick and the elderly, for example.

Even those rare organizations that have succeeded in achieving their goals rarely choose to fold up their tents and go home. Far more common is the pivot to new horizons. When diseases are cured or legislative battles are won, the nonprofits that existed to advance these causes tend not to shut down. Instead, they move the goalposts, finding new problems to solve and new causes to advocate. There is even a name for this phenomenon: the March of Dimes syndrome.

Founded in the 1930s to fight polio, the March of Dimes can justifiably claim some of the credit for ending the polio epidemic. But the end of polio did not mean the end of the March of Dimes, which continues to raise millions each year to combat a different enemy: birth defects.[11]

There are understandable reasons why groups like the March of Dimes make this kind of move. After all, nonprofits have assets and employees and supporters. Who wants to disappoint them? It's a surprisingly painful job to shut down operations.

Nonetheless, some successful organizations have chosen to do exactly that. For example, after six years of work, Out2Play, an organization that sought to create playgrounds for children in New York City public elementary schools, decided that they had effectively run out of potential locations. According to Robert Daum, their board chairman, "We just decided to declare victory and go home. Money is a scarce resource, and there are lots of other good causes out there, so there is no point in hitting up our friends and contacts for gifts simply to perpetuate the organization."[12]

Some organizations are taking the idea one step further and planning for their own obsolescence. For example, PSLF.nyc was a campaign to encourage nonprofit workers to take advantage of the federal Public Service Loan Forgiveness program. With a staff of six, they estimate that they helped 50,000 people use a special waiver to access $3 billion in loan forgiveness. According to Rich Leimsider, who conceived of the initiative:

> We essentially built a pop-up nonprofit.... During our first staff call, I said to the team that we are never going to have a retreat. We are not going to be investing a lot in our team culture. We all just need to be ready to get this stuff done and then we're going to be hopefully really proud of what we did and we're

> going to disband. And that was pretty much what happened. I think it was also refreshing for our funders. . . . It was really appealing for me to say, "I am never, ever coming back for more funding for this. I'm really just asking for one check. We're going to do something incredible together and you don't have to worry that I'm going to be added to your portfolio for the next three years."[13]

Leimsider decided that the advantages of speed outweighed the benefits of stability. In an age of social unrest, where operating a nonprofit has become increasingly difficult, this is a model that more social entrepreneurs should consider.

Chapter 9

Leadership Transition

Deciding to leave my job as the executive director of the Center for Court Innovation was a gut-wrenching choice. I had been part of a small team that created the agency in 1996, and then I served as the organization's executive director for nearly two decades. A big part of my identity and self-worth was wrapped up in my job. By the time I was through, I had spent basically half of my life at the organization. I believed in my bones that it was a special place, a unique force for good in the world. I worked alongside colleagues that I liked and admired, many of whom had become close friends. Stepping away from all of that was not a move I made lightly.

But make it I did, announcing my resignation in October 2019 and then formally leaving, with impeccable timing, on March 13, 2020, just as the pandemic was shutting down normal life.

I decided to leave for a host of reasons, but a big factor was that I had come to the conclusion that someone else could do the job better than me. That person turned out to be Courtney Bryan, who continues to shepherd the organization, now renamed the Center for Justice Innovation.

Over the course of my tenure, the organization had grown substantially. By the time I left, the annual budget was nearly $80 million and we had more than 600 staffers. The days when I knew everyone who worked at the Center for Court Innovation had long passed. Indeed, every day the organization was doing things that I didn't know about or fully understand.

What the organization needed from its leader was changing. It felt like the organization was asking me to be primarily a fundraiser and a public face—the parts of the job that I enjoyed the least. The politics of the field of criminal justice were also shifting in ways that felt inhospitable to me, becoming more left-wing and identitarian.

So I made the hard choice to step down, even though I had no idea what I wanted to do next. I was young enough (52 years old when I made the decision) that retirement was not an option. As part of the negotiations over my departure, I asked to remain on at the organization for several months in a part-time capacity (with a substantially reduced salary), which would give me the runway I needed to look for other work even as I helped with the transition to a new leader.

As the search for my successor unfolded, I was so wrapped up in my own complicated feelings that I was unprepared for the torrent of emotions that my decision unleashed in other people. Anger. Betrayal. Confusion. Excitement. It seemed like no one in my orbit at the Center for Court Innovation had a mild reaction.

In retrospect, I suppose that makes sense: we were all emotionally invested in our work and in each other. Still, at the time, I was caught off guard by the intensity and by the need to spend a lot of one-on-one time with people talking about their hopes and fears about the future. Tears were shed. Voices were raised in anger. I was the cause of a big disruption and a lot of people didn't like it.

I was also unprepared for what it would feel like to be an observer of the search process for my successor. While I did not have a formal role in the process, I helped to choose the search firm and all the board members who were making the decisions. I also knew many of the applicants for the job. Inevitably, shards of information would come to me as people shared gossip.

With the benefit of hindsight this now seems obvious, but when I was going through it, I didn't realize that all the candidates for the job would inevitably end up defining themselves against me. Which meant that each of them, whether intentionally or not, was offering a critique of my leadership and highlighting the ways that they would do better than I had. The search firm we hired to organize the process also solicited feedback from staff, asking them what they wanted in a new leader that was different from what I brought. All in all, this was not the victory lap that I had fantasized about when I contemplated my final months in the job.

Still, I got through it, and so did the organization. While I definitely made mistakes along the way, all things considered, it was a successful transition. The organization is thriving under new leadership. And I have found a new institutional home with Vital City that is better tailored to my strengths and interests. But even this objectively positive leadership transition brought with it lots of bumpy moments. It was emotionally turbulent. There was turnover: numerous people ended up leaving the Center. Many relationships were profoundly altered. My principal takeaway? There is no leadership transition without pain.

***

One of the most consistent complaints of the past several years within the nonprofit sector is that too many organizations are led by "old white guys"—Baby Boomers clinging on to power well past their sell-by date. The desire for younger and more diverse leadership is understandable and appropriate. But it is also true that institutional memory is incredibly important, and that it would be catastrophic to many organizations if their long-serving leaders were to resign tomorrow.

The decision to leave is an underappreciated act of leadership. Many nonprofit leaders have spoiled their legacies by staying too long at the party, doing real damage to their agencies in the process. But leaving too hastily has its costs too. A departure that hasn't been well thought-out and orchestrated can create organizational chaos, setting up the succeeding CEO for failure.

Bad leadership transitions are legion in the nonprofit sector. There are stories of departing CEOs who actively tried to sabotage their successors, of nonprofit boards who had no clue about how to conduct a search, and of newly hired executives who were unprepared for all the responsibilities that go with nonprofit leadership and quickly flamed out.

When is the right time for a leader to leave? How can leaders best prepare themselves and their organizations for the turbulence that transition almost always brings?

Answering these questions is crucial to the long-term health of the nonprofit sector. In the aftermath of the Covid pandemic, the sector has seen a wave of leaders exiting their jobs. *Fortune* reports that there has been an "executive suite version of the Great Resignation," with CEO departures up nearly 50% in 2023 from the year before.[1] Government and the nonprofit sector topped the list for CEO turnover. *The Chronicle of Philanthropy* declared the exodus a "great leadership upheaval." According to Gayle Brandel of PNP Staffing Group, a nonprofit executive search firm, "We've been around for 26 years, and I haven't seen anything like this."[2]

The stakes are particularly high because many of the new nonprofit CEOs coming into power will be Black and Hispanic. "Leaders of color, we are the folks that people want," says Sharyanne McSwain of Echoing Green. "When C-suite positions open, I think boards are definitely coming out saying, 'Hey, we need a leader of color for this particular institution.'"[3]

The whole sector wants and needs the next generation of nonprofit leaders to succeed. But it won't be easy. As the previous chapters have enumerated, the obstacles to successful nonprofit management have proliferated in recent years. A bad hand-off from one leader to the next will only add to the difficulty. Unfortunately, the evidence suggests that very few nonprofits are actively thinking about these issues. A 2018 survey by the Concord Leadership Group documented that less than one in four nonprofits has created a formal succession plan.[4]

In my view, the recipe for successful transition has two essential ingredients: graceful exit strategies for departing executives and intensive support for incoming CEOs.

EGO AND MONEY

One of the great things about being a nonprofit executive director is that your personal professional ambitions and the needs of your organization are often in perfect alignment. If your work is featured on television or if you write a successful grant proposal, your organization wins too. What is good for you tends to be good for the organization (and vice versa).

Of course, this is not always the case. The decision to step down (or not) is a moment when it is easy for a leader's needs and their organization's needs to slip out of sync. Good stewardship demands that a nonprofit executive be mindful of this misalignment and prioritize their organization over themselves as much as possible.

If you catch them in an unguarded moment, many nonprofit executive directors will acknowledge that it is possible to grow stale in a leadership role and that change at the top can be healthy for an organization. "Every situation is different, of course, but I'm not sure people should stay in these jobs longer than ten years or so," says Beth Goldman, the former executive director of the New York Legal Assistance Group. "When leaders become entrenched, that's when you get petty corruption and a real sense of distance between leaders and those doing the work on the ground."

And yet many nonprofit leaders desperately hold onto their jobs for as long as they can. Once they have reached the summit of organizational life, it is not unusual for nonprofit leaders to stay there for decades. When her board first approached her about developing a succession plan, Ruth Messinger, who for many years served as CEO of American Jewish World Services, had a succinct response: "I told them that the only way I was leaving my office was feet first."[5]

Messinger is far from an outlier. Nonprofit leaders stay in their jobs over the long haul for many reasons. For some, it is a failure of imagination—they cannot conceive of another job that would be as fulfilling as the one they have. Others are kept in place by ambition—they see an achievable target just around the corner and are determined to last long enough to reach it.

Every leader is unique and each organization is different, so it is difficult to articulate rules that apply to everyone. But there are two factors that pop up again and again as long-tenured leaders contemplate whether to stay or go. Unfortunately, they are also two things that are difficult for nonprofit leaders to discuss in public in an honest way: ego and money.

It takes a certain amount of self-regard to be a leader. Even as I extol the importance of humility in leaders, I also acknowledge that it is difficult to lead people or articulate a compelling organizational vision without a certain degree of personal swagger.

Very few nonprofit executives are household names. Still, in the small worlds in which they operate, nonprofit CEOs are high status. If their organization has offices, they usually have the biggest one. They are used to making, or being consulted on, every big decision.

It is not so much that executive directors come to expect a certain amount of deference (although that has traditionally been one of the perks of the job), it is more that they get accustomed to being necessary. It is hard to walk away from the feeling of being needed, of being important. Just ask Celine Coggins.

Coggins founded a nonprofit called Teach Plus that sought to build the leadership capacity of teachers. After mulling the decision for almost two years, she decided to announce that she planned to move on. Almost immediately, she noticed a profound shift within her organization. According to Coggins,

> I'd given away 100 percent of my power in a single act, and it took losing it to see what I'd had. In a matter of days, *my* inner circle was not *the* inner circle at Teach Plus. The people I would have chosen to become politically powerful didn't, the emerging queen bee of the transition bypassed me when she talked to the board, and the board took on a greater role in making high-level decisions I once owned. These were the people who agreed to take charge of my baby and get it safely to the other side. I was immensely grateful to them, but there was some anger and hurt along the way. So, was I just expected to report to work each day at the company I founded and not be in charge?! The simple answer was yes, but knowing that intellectually and knowing how it feels day-in and day-out in practice are very different.[6]

For those leaders who are not retiring, the trick is to find another job that makes them feel as vital as the one they are leaving. The problem is that it is exceedingly difficult to look for another job while simultaneously fulfilling the responsibilities of running an organization. Indeed, it can be particularly destabilizing for an organization when its leader is publicly searching for new work. Morale plummets. Donations shrink. Forward momentum grinds to a halt.

But finding a new home where a nonprofit leader will be valued is only half of the battle. Many nonprofit CEOs stay in their jobs for a straightforward reason: they need the money. They have mortgages and college tuitions to pay. They have 401k plans that they need to grow. The prospect of finding another job that pays them what they are currently making is daunting. And so they effectively retire in place. They continue to do the job, but without the same spark that made them successful in the first place. When this happens, nonprofit organizations become less effective and the progress of emerging leaders is stymied.

How can we address this situation? Is it possible to imagine a world in which long-serving nonprofit directors move on when the time is ripe?

The answer will vary from organization to organization and from leader to leader. But whatever it looks like, it must take the twin challenges of ego and money into consideration. The conventional wisdom in the nonprofit sector has long been that when leaders depart, they should cut all ties to their organization. This bit of conventional wisdom makes a certain amount of sense; after all, there are numerous examples of nonprofit CEOs attempting to inappropriately involve themselves in the ongoing work of their agencies long after their departures.

But perhaps a clean break isn't the best way to go. Survey research by the Bridgespan Group suggests that almost half of nonprofits create some sort of continuing role for organizational founders after they step down. Indeed, the Bridgespan research suggests that these organizations tend to do better than organizations that make a clean break with their long-serving leaders.[7]

There are myriad ways that organizations can ease CEOs out of their leadership roles while also finding them landing spots that are commensurate with their status and financial needs. Departing CEOs can become organizational ambassadors or fundraisers or senior fellows charged with delivering discrete intellectual projects. None of this comes for free, of course, but the money will be well spent if it enables aging nonprofit leaders a graceful exit strategy so that they can make way and help support the next generation of leaders.

"DO I REALLY WANT TO DO THIS?"

Easing the departures of exiting leaders is only half the battle of course. The other half is finding their replacements and ensuring that they succeed. In any given hierarchy, you might expect that many people would be eager to rise to the top spot. But, increasingly, that's not the case within the nonprofit sector.

In 2019, Christa Gannon decided it was time to step down from the Bay Area nonprofit she had founded and led for nearly 20 years, Fresh Lifelines for Youth (FLY). She had a ready-made replacement in mind—her chief operating officer, Ali Knight. There was just one problem: when Gannon told Knight of her plans, his immediate response was ambivalent. "I had to ask myself, 'Do I really want to do this?' There were pros and cons," says Knight.[8] Knight eventually signed on, and FLY transitioned to a working arrangement where Knight served as CEO and Gannon remained at the organization as an ambassador and fundraiser.

Unfortunately, Knight is far from alone in expressing reluctance about running a nonprofit organization. When the Building Movement Project surveyed more than 3,000 nonprofit workers in 2022 and compared the results to a similar survey in 2016, they reached a dispiriting conclusion: fewer people want to lead nonprofits. Both white respondents and people of color expressed less interest in leadership in 2022 than they had in 2016.[9]

Many Black nonprofit executives are finding that leadership is something different than what they bargained for. According to Chris Watler, the executive vice president of the Center for Employment Opportunities, a national nonprofit that provides employment opportunities to the formerly incarcerated: "A lot of people of color come into executive director jobs with serious programmatic experience and many other executive-level skills, but they don't always travel in the same social circles as board members or donors. Given this reality, a big question for me is whether boards will support learning and growth for leaders of color in the same way they have for the current leaders that board members might personally have more in common with."

Rich Leimsider, the former head of PSLF.nyc, whom we met in the last chapter, seconds this emotion. "It definitely seems harder to come in as a new nonprofit CEO these days," says Leimsider. "And I particularly worry that leaders of color are being set up for failure by majority-white nonprofit boards who congratulate themselves for the hire but don't create conditions for success."

Writing in the *Stanford Social Innovation Review,* Chanda Causer compared becoming a nonprofit executive director to the Black mayors who rose to power in the 1960s, inheriting cities hollowed out by crime and white flight. According to Causer, "For executives of color, nonprofit leadership is a 'Hollow Prize.'"[10]

The analogy between running a nonprofit and managing a city is a provocative one. Back in 1961, Nathan Glazer posed a fundamental question: Is New York City ungovernable? In a similar mode, we might ask if today's nonprofits have become effectively ungovernable, not just for people of color, but for anybody.

Back when Glazer first raised the question of ungovernability, in *Commentary* magazine, he thought that part of the answer was to attract remarkable people to the job of running cities: "Our need is for disrupters of the organizations, men who can batter the bureaucracies and make them respond to the real problems rather than to their own internal pressures and pulls, men who can open things up and let in air and light."[11]

No doubt, it would be great if nonprofits could hire executives of courage, integrity, and ambition who have the force of personality to tame the unruly bureaucracies that they inherit. People of these qualities are likely to succeed no matter what the playing field looks like. But we must also make nonprofit leadership doable by normal, un-heroic people. How can we set up newly hired executive directors, many of them people of color, to succeed?

Successful leadership transitions require a number of important constituencies to actively engage in supporting the new CEO:

Nonprofit Boards: Being on a nonprofit board can be a confusing experience. On the one hand, it is generally an honor to be asked to serve. It typically means that you have achieved a level of success in your career, that your reputation is solid, and that the organization in question thinks that an association with you will make them look good. Often you are treated with deference by the organization's staff (including its CEO), who think of you in some vague way as their boss.

But then come the expectations. You are expected to reach into your pocket (or your rolodex) to contribute money to support the organization. And you are also expected to engage in effective governance, including ensuring that the organization's money is spent wisely, that the executive director is competent, that the strategic vision is clearly articulated, and that the organization is making steady progress toward achieving it. That sounds like a full-time job. But very few board members have that kind of time to devote to an organization. Many are just showing up to a handful of meetings each year. And many have no direct experience in the work of the organization and little ability to truly understand the ecosystem in which the organization exists.

The bottom line is that there is often a mismatch between what organizations expect from boards and what they can reasonably deliver. Moments of transition often throw this reality into stark relief. Many boards effectively delegate selection of a new leader to the organization's departing executive director. Others do step up and perform their allotted role in selecting a new leader but then they step back, exhausted, and allow the new leader to sink or swim on their own. This can be a particularly damaging dynamic if the new leader is a person of color replacing a long-serving white executive director.

It would be great if every board of directors could be the platonic ideal, capable of leading a search process, attracting strong candidates, and offering the necessary support to both the departing and the entering leader. In the real world, very few boards are capable of this. Given this reality, the best thing a board can do is to be clear, honest, and realistic about what they can and cannot do as part of a leadership transition. This may not make things materially better, but it will reduce the potential for confusion and disappointment down the road.

Funders: Many foundations have traditionally taken a "wait and see" attitude when a new leader comes into an organization. This is understandable—funders want to make sure that the organization will continue to stay true to its mission and perform at the same level of excellence. Unfortunately, pausing or withholding resources at this crucial juncture in the life of an organization has all sorts of negative side effects. In particular, it amounts to essentially a vote of no confidence in a new leader at exactly the moment when they need to be delivering early and visible wins to bolster their credibility with board, staff, and clients. Instead of retreating during leadership transitions, wherever possible foundations should be stepping forward, making multi-year commitments to nonprofits and offering special funds to facilitate key aspects of the move (including underwriting coaching for new leaders and exit strategies for departing executives).

Incoming Leaders: My advice to incoming leaders is simple: Try not to complain. It is tough to be a nonprofit executive. Indeed, I have written this whole book to make the case that it has basically become an impossible job. No doubt you will have less support than you might like or than you deserve. This includes do-nothing board members, indifferent foundation officers, and ungrateful staffers. Nevertheless, it is difficult to manage the grievances of others if you are busy airing grievances of your own. Good stewardship often demands stoicism.

Staff: The message to staffers is also simple: Cut your new bosses some slack. Give them time to bed in. Don't expect them to transform the organization overnight. By all means, if your new executive director is engaged in abusive or inappropriate behavior, that should be called out. But if they simply have a different opinion than you do about, say, the war in Gaza, perhaps you could give them a break.

Exiting Leaders: Lots of leadership transition advice for departing executives focuses on technical details—how to write a good job description for your successor, who should be on a search committee, what kind of timelines yield the best results, etcetera.

All of that is fine, as far as it goes, but the truth is that the hard part of leaving a nonprofit is managing the complicated, unruly emotions that the process invariably unleashes. This is a point highlighted by a review of nonprofit transitions conducted for the consulting firm Deloitte. According to the authors, Dana O'Donovan and Jarasa Kanok, "Even the language leaders use in describing their experiences—'it's like dropping my baby off at the fire station' or 'it's like my best friend is now dating my ex'—dramatizes the gulf between the orderly activities laid out in a transition plan and the somewhat messy, human interactions that are the actual work of leadership transition."[12]

Taking your leave is hard, no doubt, but every leader must do it eventually. Picking the right moment and executing the decision in a way that minimizes disruption and maximizes the chances of success for whoever follows you is one of the most important things a nonprofit executive can do.

Unfortunately, given the increased difficulty of running a nonprofit in a time of unrest, a nonprofit leader's duty to their organization may not end with the hiring of their replacement. For decades, nonprofit leaders have been counseled to make themselves scarce after they step down. Our current moment may demand the opposite. If emerging nonprofit executives, many of them people of color, are finding it challenging to come to grips with their new jobs, the easiest remedy is to engage their predecessors in helping them. Executive coaches can play a valuable role as sounding board and thought partner, but because each nonprofit agency is so unique, no one's advice and support will be more valuable than someone who knows the personalities and retains a measure of institutional memory about how and why the organization has evolved in the way it has.

This won't work in every case, of course. Sometimes the right thing to do is to distance the organization from the departing executive. But these cases tend to be the exception, not the rule. As Bridgespan found when they studied the issue, the most successful leadership transitions tend not to involve clean breaks. The Bridgespan study was specifically focused on departing founders, but really the idea applies to any departing executive. According to the researchers, "We distilled four conditions to guide an organization that is considering an extended founder role: First, the founder has the capability and desire to stay engaged. Second, the board perceives clear value from the founder staying involved. Third, the founder is willing to play a different role and genuinely wants the successor to succeed. And fourth, the successor is willing to work with the founder. All require both founder and successor to sublimate ego."[13]

And so we return to where we began: with the problem of ego. In moderation, ego can be a spur to achievement, helping a leader raise money, set ambitious goals, and generate staff loyalty. Taken too far, however, ego is the enemy of effective leadership and the saboteur of smooth transition. Where is the line between healthy and destructive ego? According to Robert Greenleaf, the inventor of servant leadership,

> Ego focuses on one's own survival, pleasure, and enhancement to the exclusion of others; ego is selfishly ambitious. It sees relationships in terms of threat or no threat, like little children who classify all people as "nice" or "mean." Conscience, on the other hand, both democratizes and elevates ego to a larger sense of the group, the whole, the community, the greater good. It sees life in terms of service and contribution, in terms of others' security and fulfillment.[14]

In the end, all parties to a leadership transition—not just the outgoing and the incoming leader, but staff and board members and funders too—should heed this wisdom, tempering ego with conscience and focusing on the greater good.

Conclusion

The Challenge of Accountability

In 2024, the journal *American Affairs* published a jeremiad linking nonprofits to the decline of American cities. In "The Nonprofit Industrial Complex and the Corruption of the American City," writer Jonathan Ireland accuses nonprofits of being false-flag operations that seek to undermine the greater good:

> Consider the word "nonprofit." Whoever came up with the idea of calling these organizations "nonprofits" was a marketing genius on the level of Steve Jobs. When someone hears the word nonprofit, they assume that such an organization is working for the public good; that it serves the homeless, protects the weak, exists for the benefit and the betterment of society at large. Hearing that something is a "nonprofit" immediately gives a sense that the organization is trustworthy and the people running it are driven by a charitable agenda. It's a word that shuts down the critical faculties and grants an instantaneous moral stature to any organization to which it is applied. Consequently, nonprofits receive a benefit of the doubt that would not be granted to any other form of private corporation. Yet nonprofit organizations are frequently the exact opposite of what they appear to be. As a consequence of the benefit of the doubt provided to nonprofits, there is rarely enough oversight to guarantee that they are doing what we pay them to do. In

> some cities, upwards of a billion dollars of public funds are paid to nonprofit organizations every year with glaringly insufficient safeguards to ensure that the money is used in a manner likely to serve the public interest.[1]

Nonprofit leaders might be tempted to dismiss Ireland's argument as the provocative, but ultimately harmless, venting of an aggrieved conservative, but they shouldn't. Because it's not a one-off. Indeed, Ireland is part of a growing chorus asking hard questions about the nonprofit sector.

Arguments against nonprofits are being launched from many directions these days.

From business: venture capitalist Garry Tan, the CEO of Y Combinator claims that "Nonprofits are bad. We need to bring back high integrity state capacity, highly paid, chosen for merit and held to high standards of accountability. The state must end its practice of farming out state capacity to feckless nonprofits that grift and are not held to any standard."[2]

From academia: left-wing professor Claire Dunning writes, "Of the many myths about the United States, few rival the longevity of the supposed independence of the voluntary or charitable realm: the idea that nonprofit organizations stand apart from both the state and market . . . the nonprofit sector, far from being independent, serves to reinforce the status quo and discipline efforts to disrupt it."[3]

From journalism: *The Spectator* editor Melissa Chen argues "There's a strong case to be made that the NGO-Industrial Complex is actually more harmful than the Military-Industrial Complex."[4]

Each of these detractors of the nonprofit sector has their own axe to grind, but at the root of all of their critiques is the challenge of accountability.

STAFF UNREST AND THE DONOR-OCRACY

Businesses are subject to the brutal logic of the marketplace—if they cannot attract enough paying customers, they will go belly up. Government agencies don't go bankrupt, but if the public is unhappy with their performance, they can vote in new leaders in an effort to change things. As rough as they are, these are mechanisms of public accountability that help ensure the usefulness of the private and public sectors.

Who are nonprofits accountable to? The answer is complex. Broadly speaking, nonprofit organizations are meant to be accountable to the public—after all, they receive a special tax-exempt status on the supposition that they are serving the public interest. In addition, nonprofits should also be accountable to their boards, donors, community partners, staff members, clients, and volunteers. In the best-case scenario, you could make the argument that nonprofits are among the most highly accountable institutions imaginable, with numerous stakeholders capable of exerting collective pressure to ensure good performance.

But reality often tells a different story. Recent years have seen some spectacular examples of bad behavior in nonprofit institutions. A few cases in point:

- The leader of Raheem AI, a nonprofit that seeks to promote police accountability, was accused of failing to deliver a promised technology application and of spending tens of thousands of dollars of the agency's money on clothing.[5]
- GLAAD, a leading LGBTQ nonprofit, paid for its chief executive to travel in first class style at luxury hotels, including a stay in a seven-bedroom chalet in Switzerland that cost nearly half a million dollars to rent for the week.[6]

- The head of a charity called Modest Needs was charged with embezzling $2.5 million to, among other things, rent a Manhattan apartment, have cosmetic surgery, and dine at expensive restaurants.[7]
- Funds raised by the Black Lives Matter Global Network Foundation were used to buy a house in California for nearly $6 million.[8]

And these are just stories from a single newspaper (the *New York Times*)!

(The *Times* thinks that there is enough malfeasance within the nonprofit sector that they have dedicated a reporter, David Fahrenthold, to cover the field. In announcing the new beat, Fahrenthold wrote: "I cover nonprofits. Who should I investigate next? The *Times* is looking for your tips about lawbreaking, self-enrichment and influence-peddling in the nonprofit world."[9])

The media can play an important role in holding nonprofits to account, but they can only do so much. There are thousands of nonprofits, after all, and only so many of them are prominent or impactful or scandalous enough to merit news coverage.

In truth, very few nonprofit leaders actively worry about being the subject of investigative journalism. Nor do they fear government intervention. The Internal Revenue Service requires nonprofit agencies to file an IRS Form 990 each year, containing basic financial information about revenues and expenditures. The IRS has the right to revoke an organization's tax-exempt status, although this happens infrequently. Nonprofits are also subject to some regulation at the state and local level, but this is generally light touch. And, of course, nonprofit executives can be prosecuted by local district attorneys if they engage in criminal behavior. But most nonprofit leaders can go their entire careers without hearing from any of these public agencies.

On a day-to-day basis, the two forces of accountability that nonprofit executives think about the most are their staffs and their donors.

As we have seen throughout this book, we are living in an age of culture war disruption and staff unrest. Thanks to social media and new technologies, it is easier than ever for nonprofit employees to organize themselves and to make a public fuss when they are unhappy. They have availed themselves of this opportunity repeatedly over the past several years. This has had some salutary effects. Thanks to staff advocacy, there has been pressure for nonprofits to root out sexual abusers, to improve working conditions, and to think more deeply about racial justice.

But nonprofits make a massive error if they come to overemphasize the importance of pleasing their staff members.

In a 2023 press release announcing a new initiative designed to get nonprofits to listen to the voices of their employees, the Ford Foundation claimed that workers want their employers to "prioritize their employees as *the most important* stakeholder" (emphasis mine).[10] Making employees the most important stakeholder may make sense to employees, but the primary answer to the question "Who should nonprofits serve?" cannot possibly be "their employees." That way lies madness. Nonprofits do not, and should not, exist to serve the needs of their staff members. In order to merit public trust, nonprofits must always put their mission first.

If staffers are the primary internal influencer of nonprofit behavior, the most significant external oversight of nonprofit agencies tends to come directly from their funders.

In ways both obvious and subtle, the relationship between donor and grantee is profoundly unequal. Powerful donors end up exerting enormous influence over the behavior of nonprofits. (Indeed, the quickest way to figure out what a nonprofit is all about is to look at its list of funders.)

If public accountability is an issue for nonprofits, it is an even bigger problem for organized philanthropy. Who elected these people? And why does their wealth entitle them to a greater say than the rest of us in the fate of our society?

The left may abhor the philanthropy of the Koch Brothers and the right may vilify the donations of George Soros, but, right or left, funders share something in common, according to former foundation executive Jeff Cain: "Liberal or conservative, the professional philanthropic class shares a fundamentally progressive belief that it can design America and Americans from above: Salvation comes by way of experts and elites, top down, not bottom up."[11]

From one perspective, foundations are an important bulwark against government overreach and an incubator of social innovation. Viewed from another, they are a symptom of a broken society, the legacy of an unfair social order that enriches the haves at the expense of the have-nots.

It is not my purpose here to settle the debate over private philanthropy. Rather, I seek simply to make the case that foundations wield an outsized influence on the nonprofit sector. Foundations can, at a whim, force their grantees to adopt metrics or DEI initiatives or any other new idea that strikes their fancy as a grant requirement. Even when grants don't come with explicit conditions for nonprofits, there are often invisible strings attached. Nonprofits intuitively understand that there would be real consequences if they were to carve out positions that their paymasters disagree with.

Over the past 50 years, as new billionaires have been minted and new mega foundations have emerged to disperse their charitable giving, the balance of power between philanthropy and the nonprofit sector has tilted even more in the direction of the donor class. One reason for this, according to Marshall Ganz, a lecturer at Harvard's Kennedy School of Government, is the disappearance of membership associations (a development that we explored in Chapter 3, when we looked at the problem of polarization in the nonprofit sector.) Ganz argues that

> Self-governing membership associations funded by their membership and accountable to them have become scarce as hen's teeth. They have largely been replaced by nonprofits neither financially nor politically accountable to members who don't exist. They are, rather, accountable to the wealthy who fund them—their donors. This "donor-ocracy," has flourished in the last 40 years. It's been a radical transformation. It sustains organizations which claim to represent a community not because the community elected them, not because the community pays for them, but because a donor likes them. As such, a whole system of ersatz representation has been constructed.[12]

Private funders are not the only ones who throw their weight around, of course. Government exerts its own power over the nonprofit sector. Government often drives a hard bargain in its dealings with the nonprofit sector, taking advantage of the idealism and mission-driven nature of nonprofits. For example, many government funders sharply limit the amount of overhead they will support, drastically reducing a nonprofit's ability to pay for rent and other general expenses. Government funders, eager to show the public that they are not wasting taxpayer money, often select the lowest bid when sifting through proposals, which places significant downward pressure on nonprofit salaries. And, as Claire Dunning and others have pointed out, few government agencies are interested in actively funding the revolution; for understandable reasons, nonprofits that criticize the mayor typically have a hard time getting funding from the mayor's office.

Viewed more positively, many public and private funders actively review the fiscal and programmatic performance of their grantees and withdraw support from those who do not meet their standards. In general, that's a good thing—nonprofits should have to deliver on their promises (or have good reasons for not doing so).

At least in theory, board governance is another tool for positively shaping the behavior of nonprofits. And sometimes things do work that way—there are definitely some nonprofits that have vibrant, involved boards that help them to chart direction and assess performance. But many boards are unable (or unwilling) to perform these functions. Some are simply disengaged. Others are too beholden to the organization's executive director to offer meaningful oversight. Still others lack the necessary expertise. (Many boards do not include anyone with experience running a nonprofit organization, tending to favor big donors and local dignitaries instead.) In reality, nonprofit boards are a flawed vehicle. They are better than nothing, but, in their current incarnation, they are, by themselves, incapable of ensuring public accountability.[13]

THE THREAT TO CIVIL SOCIETY

All of this serves as the backdrop for a deeply worrying trend. As Rachel Kleinfeld of the Carnegie Endowment for Peace has documented,

> Today, the space in which U.S. civil society operates is closing in—thanks to polarization, not a ruling party. Illiberals on the far right and far left have decided that it's not enough to persuade: They must eliminate undesirable ideas—and organizations—using whatever power is at hand, their tactics pulled straight from those used by anti-democratic regimes abroad.[14]

On the right, this illiberalism takes the form of calls to use the force of government to undermine left-leaning foundations and nonprofits. This includes efforts to cut federal funding to controversial nonprofits (e.g., Planned Parenthood), bills that seek to police ideology at American universities, and the use of Congressional oversight committees to investigate disfavored organizations. On the left, illiberal actors have used the levers of government power to spread DEI programs and worked within sympathetic institutions (e.g., universities, Facebook) to limit free speech and mute right-wing voices.

Given our polarized climate, it is not difficult to imagine a future in which the Internal Revenue Service becomes a political weapon used by Republicans and Democrats alike to go after disfavored nonprofits and foundations. We have started down this route before. During the Obama administration, when the IRS raised concerns about granting 501(c)(3) status to a few conservative groups affiliated with the Tea Party, the Republican-controlled Congress went ballistic. Following a Congressional investigation, the Obama administration threw several IRS officials under the bus in an effort to draw a line under the controversy.

In light of this history, JD Vance's threats to go after prominent nonprofits and foundations that he believes are promoting a radical left-wing ideology should be viewed with real alarm. And the logic of polarization suggests that once Republicans seize on a political tactic, Democrats are likely to follow suit.

How can we avoid this grim future? Is it possible to dispel the storm clouds of illiberalism that threaten the space for civil society in general and nonprofits in particular?

Nonprofit leaders can help beat back this threat by embracing the idea of public accountability. Too many nonprofits think of "accountability" as basically a tick-box exercise. But truly being a force for good in the world means more than filling out the necessary paperwork with the appropriate authorities or following the "best practice" guidelines issued by the Bridgespan Group or other such consultants.

As Tufts professor Alnoor Ebrahim has highlighted, "Accountability is not simply about compliance with laws or industry standards, but is more deeply connected to organizational purpose and public trust."[15] In other words, true accountability is unlikely to be achieved by oversight and sanction; external pressures to induce good behavior will only take us so far. Ideally, accountability has an internal dimension as well. Nonprofit leaders should feel a keen desire to act in a responsible fashion—and to ensure that their agencies are truly serving the public by addressing social problems.

What this looks like will, of course, vary from organization to organization. But nonprofit leaders should begin with a few fundamentals:

Mission comes first. This seems an obvious point, but it can't be taken for granted these days. Amid all of the various stakeholders that nonprofits must serve (board, staff, community partners, funders, etc.), the public should be at the top of the list.

This means putting staff issues in perspective. Nonprofits should absolutely take the concerns of staff seriously and seek to create working environments where people are treated well and paid fairly, but staff cannot be the ones steering the ship. Nonprofit executives would be well-advised to look for ways to solicit input from their teams and factor employee voice into decision-making, but they should not hand over control of their agencies to the staff. Leadership still matters.

Here is an area where nonprofit boards can be particularly helpful. Because they are not involved in the day-to-day management of the organization, they can avoid getting caught up in the back-and-forth between staff and management. Their distance from operations can give them some much-needed perspective, helping them resist the passions of the moment. Ideally, a board will back up a nonprofit CEO when he or she tries to keep an organization focused on its mission.

Putting mission first means that the self-interest of an organization or its staff should not come before the public good. Typically, these things are in sync—when organizations are doing well, it also means that some measure of progress is being made toward achieving their public mission. But it is possible for there to be a conflict between what's best for a nonprofit and what's in the interest of the greater good. "Nonprofits don't exist for the purpose of self-perpetuation, to ensure employment for those who work there, to make staff and/or board members feel good and pretend to be doing good," writes nonprofit consultant Laura Otten. "Thus, when an organization struggles year after year to stay afloat, or when its mission is no longer necessary or valued, or others are doing the same job only better, or any number of other scenarios, the question must be asked, 'do we still need to exist?'"[16]

Putting the public good over narrow self-interest is crucial to disarming left-wing critics of the "nonprofit industrial complex." Many of these critics are prone to point out that nonprofits haven't successfully ended poverty or eliminated racism or solved a host of other social problems despite being given tons of money over the years. But is the world a better or a worse place due to the efforts of nonprofits? For me, the answer to this question is easy. Nonprofits may not have solved every problem under the sun, but they have made real progress in any number of areas and helped to ameliorate many of the worst aspects of our society.

If nonprofits haven't successfully created utopia on earth, it is not because they are self-dealing frauds, co-opted by their government partners and rich donors. Rather, it is because no one actually knows how to solve problems like poverty and racism and inequality without producing damaging side effects that reasonable people might seek to avoid. Nor is there broad public support in the United States for the kinds of massive structural changes (and tax increases) that might help make a dent in solving these kinds of problems. Nonprofits are, by and large, doing the best they can given these realities.

Do DEI differently. With a few exceptions, nonprofits should look to sidestep the culture wars. In general, nonprofits should seek to speak to the entire American public, not just progressives or MAGA Republicans. To do this effectively means minimizing the use of polarizing language and ideas. As currently constructed, "DEI" is the epitome of both.

Rather than spending precious time and energy fighting for the DEI status quo ante, nonprofits should switch gears, testing out new vocabulary and new approaches for promoting diversity in the workplace. In particular, this should include abandoning mandatory diversity trainings and avoiding "race-conscious" policies that may violate civil rights law.

Invest in mentoring. Mentoring is one of the most important things that nonprofit leaders can do to develop the next generation of leadership, both for their organization and the sector at large. According to Frank Dobbin and Alexandra Kalev, the authors of *Getting to Diversity,* it is also one of the best ways to advance diversity within an organization. They see mentoring as a way to help give people of color and other underrepresented groups the kind of professional networks they need to succeed. To make it work, according to Kalev,

> You want to match based on interest. . . . Probably the most important reason to match by interest is that you want the relationships to break down the segregation, those glass walls between people like white men, for example, and women or people of color. You want to create matches that are actually cross-cultural, but based on interests, because that's what we do in organizations: we work in functions like finance or AI, based on disciplines or interests.[17]

Know when it is time to go. This book has attempted to detail some of the ways in which the nonprofit playing field has shifted in recent years—and how nonprofit leaders might adapt. Many will successfully acclimate to the new realities of life in the sector.

But some will not. There is no shame in that. (I speak from experience here—I was someone who decided I could not adapt to the changing dynamics in the sector.)

But there is shame in continuing to do the job even after your sell-by date has arrived. Nonprofit leaders should invest as much focus and care in their leave-taking as they do on their ascent up the ladder. As the example of George Washington teaches us, abdicating a position of power can be an important act of leadership—perhaps the most important. Nonprofit executives should think long and hard about whether they are truly the best people to lead their organization. If not, they should give way, for the greater good.

AN UNGUIDED SOCIAL MISSILE

Dutch Leonard is an economist with joint appointments at Harvard's business school and the Kennedy School of Government. His field of study is organizational leadership. When he was recently asked about the role of the nonprofit sector in democracy, Leonard said:

> The social sector as currently configured is something of an unguided social missile. And that's a worry. And I think in spite of that, we actually get very good work out of this sector. And so I often ask why. This is the sector that has the hardest problems (it has the problems no one else wants to deal with), and it has the least resources (because it has to get them voluntarily from third parties). It can't get them directly either through taxation nor, for the most part, through exchange transactions. So it has the hardest problems, the least resources, and no mechanism

> for accountability. And yet it does good work. How does that happen? It happens because of the individual leadership of the people in the sector whose intentions are good. They're trying to figure out what the actual problems are and are trying to find ways of being oriented towards the voices of the people they're helping. In short, the good performance is in spite of the imperfections in the structure—and is a result of the good leadership of people in the sector.[18]

This book has sought to reinforce Leonard's argument. It has tried to make the case that something has changed in recent years within the social sector—and not for the good. Leadership in the nonprofit space has always been difficult, but the challenges have become even more intense as a new generation has entered the workforce, as polarization has gripped the country, and as demands for racial justice have proliferated. These forces (and others) have buffeted the nonprofit sector. Many of our nonprofit organizations are the weaker for it—less cohesive, less stable, and, ultimately, less effective.

The foibles of any individual nonprofit are of little consequence in the grand scheme of things. But the slow, steady drip of negative news coming out of the sector in recent years—from the cases of corruption to the overpaid executives to the staff implosions—does gradually begin to take a toll. The modest, but significant, reductions in public trust tracked by the Independent Sector are one sign of this.

Another, even more distressing, sign is the decline in the rates of Americans who volunteer or donate to charity. According to a recent report from Benjamin Soskis of the Urban Institute's Center on Nonprofits and Philanthropy, the share of U.S. households reporting donating to charity has fallen steadily of late, from more than 66% in 2000 to less than 50% in 2018.[19] Most of the decline seems to be coming from lower-level donors, meaning that more giving to nonprofit organizations is coming from the wealthy, further enhancing their influence over the sector.

The decline in voluntarism is not quite as pronounced, but the trajectory is the same: downward. According to the University of Maryland's Do Good Institute, the national adult volunteer rate peaked in 2003, with nearly 30% of adults reporting some sort of volunteer activity. By 2015, the rate had gone down to less than 25%. More recent surveys show similar numbers.[20]

Both sides of the American cultural war debate like to bash the nonprofit sector these days. To be sure, the language and the targets of right-wing activists are very different than the language and the targets favored by the left. But if you listen to the underlying music, it sounds pretty much the same. Both sides tend to suggest that the nonprofit sector is a tool of undemocratic and unaccountable elites who use the sector to advance their political goals at the expense of the people. Michael Hartmann, writing in *American Affairs,* goes so far as to suggest a political alliance between progressives and populist conservatives to remake American philanthropy, an institution "toward which both wings of our political spectrum now have deep, resentful, and growing distrust."[21]

In sum, the warning lights are flashing yellow. The crisis is upon us. Now is the time to move with purpose to strengthen trust in nonprofits. We should proceed with a healthy sense of urgency because Harvard economist Dutch Leonard is correct: amazing things are still being done every day with the help of the nonprofit sector—the hungry are being fed, children are being educated, the homeless are being housed, and so much more. This is largely due to the work of the men and women who lead these organizations, many of whom are already practicing good nonprofit stewardship rooted in values like humility, flexibility, long-term thinking, and emotional intelligence.

The nonprofit sector is a crucial component of the American experiment in liberal democracy, a fact that Daniel Patrick Moynihan recognized back in the 1980s. In a speech titled "Pluralism and the Independent Sector," Moynihan celebrated the role that "mediating institutions" play in American life as alternatives "to the all-powerful market or the all-powerful state."[22] When they are functioning properly, nonprofits are part of the connective tissue that binds us together as Americans, helping to keep a country of remarkable size and unprecedented diversity moving forward.

It will be difficult to knit our social fabric together if Americans continue to lose trust in our nonprofit institutions. In an age of social unrest and culture war churn, we need effective nonprofits—and good nonprofit leadership—now more than ever.

Epilogue

The Return of Trump

I write this just days after Donald Trump's inauguration in January of 2025.

Trump's previous electoral victory in 2016 was a signal moment in the American culture wars. With his crude behavior and his "America First" rhetoric, Trump was, in the eyes of many, the living embodiment of a society permanently stained by racism, misogyny, and xenophobia. In the name of resistance, these Americans decided to do all that they could to show the world that Trump was #NotMyPresident. Millions flooded the streets to register their objections. Civil servants exercised what I have called the "practitioner veto," employing a variety of tactics designed to obstruct Trump's desired policy changes. Many mainstream news organizations all but declared themselves part of the opposition to the new administration.

Trump's election in 2016 also reverberated powerfully throughout the nonprofit sector. In general, Trump was an accelerant of both staff unrest and a leftward ideological tilt, adding rocket fuel to two trends which predated his arrival. To do their part to advance "the Resistance," many nonprofits essentially embraced negative partisanship—anything Trump was for, they were against. This was justified, in part, because Trump had lost the popular vote and because other unusual circumstances, including allegations of Russian interference, made his election seem illegitimate to many observers.

The concerted opposition to Trump probably did make a difference, at least at the margins. Some Trump initiatives—for example, the "Muslim ban"—were delayed, at least for a time. The massive Women's March and the Black Lives Matter protests demonstrated that a significant segment of the voting public did not endorse Trump's agenda. And obstruction from federal workers succeeded in infuriating Trump, leading him to declare war on what he labeled "the deep state."

But any battles that were won along the way did not add up to victory in the larger war of public opinion. Despite the best efforts of his opponents in the media, academia, government, and the nonprofit sector, Trump managed to increase his support, ultimately winning the presidential election in 2024—and bringing with him Republican control of the House and the Senate.

According to Liam Kerr of The Welcome Party, a moderate Democratic advocacy group, "The first wave Resistance was fierce, energetic, and often righteously belligerent—a slash and burn approach to saving democracy. That may have made sense as an emotional reaction to Trumpism, but it did not win convincing majorities and does not appear poised to in the near future."[1]

Notwithstanding this reality, in the wake of Trump's reelection, many prominent voices have been calling for Resistance 2.0, essentially doubling down on the scorched earth strategy of eight years ago. After the election was called for Trump, the ACLU offered no grace note to the president-elect, just a stern warning: "We're clear-eyed about the chaos and destruction a second Trump administration will cause to our nation. That's why we're done with handwringing, admiring the problem, or waiting anxiously to see which unlawful action President-elect Trump will take on Day One. We are ready to take action the minute Trump takes the oath of office."[2]

There are good reasons why the ACLU chose to adopt a combative tone. After all, on the campaign trail, Trump made ominous noises about going after his enemies and ignoring the rule of law. The threat of mass deportations looms large.

There are particularly ominous tidings for nonprofit agencies these days. In November 2024, the Republican Congress passed legislation that some have taken to calling "the nonprofit killer bill." Among other things, the "Stop Terror-Financing and Tax Penalties on American Hostages Act" would allow the Treasury Department to strip an organization of its nonprofit status if it were deemed a "terrorism-supporting" organization. The bill passed the US House of Representatives, over the objections of many nonprofit associations, largely along partisan lines, but the congressional session ended without any action by the Senate on the legislation.

The odds would seem to be good that the bill will be taken up again by the Trump administration at some point. In the past, Vice President JD Vance has suggested that the federal government should take a hard look at foundations and nonprofits engaged in progressive political advocacy, with an eye to possibly changing their tax status. And one of Trump's first acts upon returning to office was to attempt to freeze trillions of dollars of federal funding, which included grants to thousands of nonprofit groups. The directive was ultimately rescinded in the face of legal challenges and widespread opposition, much of it organized by nonprofit groups.

If past is prologue, the nonprofit sector will need to be on high alert in the days to come. The next four years are sure to be turbulent.

But, at least at the moment that I write this, there are strong arguments to be made against a return to 2016-style resistance. Conor Friedersdorf, a writer for *The Atlantic*, argues that following this same template again would be a mistake for nonprofits and other groups, because "an opposition that purports to defend democracy cannot deny legitimacy to such a clear democratic winner." He also believes that many Americans are simply exhausted from years of obsessive focus on Trump: "unaligned Americans who don't even like Trump are tired of being browbeaten for not hating him enough."[3]

Daniel Stid, a former program officer at the Hewlett Foundation, makes the case that his fellow philanthropists should not underwrite the Resistance this time around. According to Stid, doing so would provide "MAGA enthusiasts with nearly perfect foils—wealthy and unaccountable elites based in blue coastal enclaves financing efforts to counter the people's will." He also suggests that a renewed Resistance would only serve to accelerate polarization "by fomenting an apocalyptic, fear-based politics in which the population is starkly divided into friends and enemies, darkly mirroring the Manichaean worldview of the most vociferous populists."[4]

While it is not a problem if a handful of nonprofits follow the ACLU into full-throated opposition mode, the vast majority of nonprofits would be wise to resist this urge. Indeed, I believe that many, if not all, of the organizations that embraced resistance the last time around ended up doing real long-term damage to the sector by allowing themselves to be seen as explicitly political actors. Indeed, it seems that if there is a battle for public support between Donald Trump and mainstream American institutions (government, media, nonprofits, universities, etc.), that Donald Trump is winning, at least at the moment.

According to Yascha Mounk the author of *The Great Experiment: Why Diverse Democracies Fall Apart and How They Can Endure*, the key question for anybody who wants to preserve and protect American institutions is not "Why do they like him?" but "Why do they hate us?" As Mounk has written, "Until the Democratic Party—along with the wider world of the American Establishment with which it is now deeply associated in the minds of voters—is able to give (and act on) an honest answer to that question, every clever tactic for how to resist Trump is doomed to fail."[5]

In general, politicized organizations are distrusted organizations. This is a point underlined by a recent study that looked at the perceptions of American institutions. More than three thousand survey respondents were asked their opinions about a variety of institutions—business, the media, the Army, etcetera. Findings from the study suggest that "higher perceived politicization of institutions consistently predicted lower trust, often with large effect sizes. Similar patterns were observed between institutions, such that the institutions perceived as the most politicized were also the least trusted."[6]

Provocatively, the research team found lower levels of trust in politicized institutions *even among those who shared the political slant of the institution in question*. Progressives were less willing to trust left-leaning institutions that appeared politicized. The same was true among conservatives. The researchers' conclusion was simple: "Even when ideologies align, people distrust politicized institutions."

This is a truth that Ira Glasser knows well. Glasser, who led the ACLU for more than 20 years, has recently become a vocal critic of the organization, arguing that it has strayed away from its traditional, content-neutral support for free speech in order to become a generic progressive advocacy group. (Mission creep alert!) According to Glasser, "Whether you're the ACLU or (rival civil liberties organization) FIRE, if you're going to hold Trump accountable when he exceeds the limits of his power, you cannot be in a position of being seen as anti-Trump or of having campaigned against him politically. Otherwise, you will have no credibility, and you will not be effective."[7]

The immediate problem for nonprofits may be the Trump administration, but the underlying crisis remains the same: declining public trust in the sector. The trap that Trump presents for nonprofit leaders is that, in the long run, direct opposition to him is likely to hurt the nonprofit sector more than it hurts him.

Trump's win in 2024 is itself an indicator of depressingly low levels of confidence in American institutions—clearly, concerns about the damage Trump might wreak were insufficient to motivate the majority of voters to pull the lever for Kamala Harris.

Why is trust in American institutions so low? There are many reasons. One big one is the fact that both the right (Ronald Reagan: "Government is not the solution to our problem, government is the problem") and the left (Nikole Hannah-Jones: "Our founding ideals of liberty and equality were false when they were written") have devoted so much energy to attacking American institutions in recent years.

Now, more than ever, nonprofits need good stewardship that prioritizes long-term thinking and avoids the dangers of mission creep. Nonprofit leaders who want to reduce polarization and prevent the next authoritarian threat to American democracy should take pains not to succumb to Trump derangement syndrome.

Restoring public faith in civil society and the nonprofit sector is not going to happen overnight. But it will never happen unless nonprofit leaders distance themselves, as much as is possible, from the culture wars. Going forward, it is essential that these institutions attempt to speak to *all* Americans, not just those who are already ideologically simpatico with them.

Nonprofits would also be well-advised to embrace organizational discipline. Less can be more: by remaining focused on their core mission rather than being dragged into controversies beyond their ken, nonprofits can reduce the chances that they will be viewed as politicized actors.

The best way for nonprofits to begin to address the corrosive problem of declining public trust, in sum, is to do an outstanding job of whatever their core work may be—serving the needy, educating young people, building housing, etcetera. The real, long-term enemy is not Trump—it's public cynicism. Unless that enemy is defeated, we are likely to see more presidential results like the one in 2024 in the years ahead.

ENDNOTES

Introduction

1. Alexis de Tocqueville. *Democracy in America* (New York: Bantam Books, 2000), 630–631.
2. There are technically 19 different types of nonprofit organizations in the United States. In general, this book focuses on the charitable organizations that the Internal Revenue Service deems to be tax-exempt under section 501(c)(3) of the tax code. These organizations are exempted from paying taxes because they serve a public purpose of one kind or another. While these groups may run a budget surplus in any given year, they are prohibited from distributing these revenues to shareholders or managers the way a business can. Donors to 501(c)(3) organizations are able to deduct their charitable contributions from their taxable income, which amounts to a massive (and more or less invisible) government subsidy of the nonprofit sector.
3. "The Nonprofit Sector in Brief." Urban Institute, June 18, 2020. https://nccs.urban.org/project/nonprofit-sector-brief
4. Fredrik DeBoer. *How Elites Ate the Social Justice Movement* (New York: Simon & Schuster, 2023), 98.
5. Lester Salamon, ed. *The State of Nonprofit America* (Washington, DC: Brookings Institution Press, 2012), 6.
6. Adrian Budhu. "The Nonprofit Theatre Sector Attracted 23 Million Attendees in 2020." *SMU DataArts*, November 23, 2021. https://culturaldata.org/learn/data-at-work/2021/theatre-facts-2020-theatre-communications-group/

7. To be precise, the NFL was never a 501(c)(3) charitable organization. For many years, it had a 501(c)(6) designation, which meant that it was considered a trade organization. The NFL relinquished its tax-exempt status, under public pressure, in 2015.
8. Fredrik deBoer. *How Elites Ate the Social Justice Movement* (New York: Simon & Schuster, 2023), 98.
9. INCITE! Women of Color Against Violence. *The Revolution Will Not Be Funded* (Durham: Duke University Press, 2017). https://collectiveliberation.org/wp-content/uploads/2013/01/Smith_Intro_Revolution_Will_Not_Be_Funded.pdf
10. Peter Buffet. "The Charitable-Industrial Complex." *New York Times*, July 26, 2013. https://www.nytimes.com/2013/07/27/opinion/the-charitable-industrial-complex.html
11. Mark Kramer. "Are the Elite Hijacking Social Change?" *Stanford Social Innovation Review*, Fall 2018. https://ssir.org/books/reviews/entry/are_the_elite_hijacking_social_change
12. Sophie Hayssen. "The Nonprofit Industrial Complex: What Is It and How Does It Work?" *Teen Vogue*, September 7, 2022. https://www.teenvogue.com/story/non-profit-industrial-complex-what-is
13. John O'Sullivan. "O'Sullivan's First Law." *National Review*, October 27, 1989. https://web.archive.org/web/20100715191034/http://old.nationalreview.com/flashback/flashback-jos062603.asp
14. https://www.fordfoundation.org. Accessed November 20, 2023.
15. John B. Judis and Ruy Teixeira. *Where Have All the Democrats Gone?* (New York: Henry Holt, 2023), 8.
16. It is worth noting that Judis, Teixeira, and Lind do not self-identify as conservatives. The critique they offer of nonprofit organizations is shared by many moderates and liberals.
17. "Trust in Civil Society." Independent Sector. https://independentsector.org/wp-content/uploads/2022/05/Independent-Sector-Trust-Report-2023.pdf
18. "Most Trusted Brands 2022." Morning Consult. https://go.morningconsult.com/rs/850-TAA-511/images/Most_Trusted_Brands_2022_Nonprofits.pdf

Chapter 1

1. Coleman Hughes. "A Case for Color Blindness." TED, April 2023. https://www.ted.com/talks/coleman_hughes_a_case_for_color_blindness/transcript?language=en
2. "More Americans Disapprove Than Approve of Colleges Considering Race, Ethnicity in Admissions Decisions." Pew Research Center, June 8, 2023. https://www.pewresearch.org/politics/2023/06/08/more-americans-disappro

ve-than-approve-of-colleges-considering-race-ethnicity-in-admissions-decisions/

3. Coleman Hughes. "Why Is TED Scared of Color Blindness?" Coleman's Corner, September 28, 2023. https://colemanhughes.substack.com/p/why-is-ted-scared-of-color-blindness
4. Chris Anderson (@TEDChris). "Turns out There Are a Few More Things I Need to Say . . ." X, September 29, 2023. https://twitter.com/TEDchris/status/1707817509905187143. Accessed October 17, 2024.
5. Michael Dimock. "5 Things to Keep in Mind When You Hear About Gen Z, Millennials, Boomers and Other Generations." Pew Research Center. May 22, 2023. https://www.pewresearch.org/short-reads/2023/05/22/5-things-to-keep-in-mind-when-you-hear-about-gen-z-millennials-boomers-and-other-generations/
6. Isobel Lewis. "Jodie Foster Divides Fans With Comments About 'Really Annoying' Generation Z." *Independent.* January 8, 2024. https://au.news.yahoo.com/jodie-foster-divides-fans-comments-144128953.html
7. Dene More. "Generations Expert Jean Twenge Busts Some Myths About Boomers, Gen X, Millennials and Gen Z." Zed. May 4, 2023. https://everythingzoomer.com/zed-book-club/2023/05/04/generations-expert-jean-twenge-busts-some-myths-about-boomers-gen-x-millennials-and-gen-z/
8. "Educational Attainment Distribution in the United States from 1960 to 2022." Statista, August 22, 2024. https://www.statista.com/statistics/184260/educational-attainment-in-the-us/
9. Matt Grossman and David A. Hopkins. *Polarized by Degrees: How the Diploma Divide and the Culture War Transformed American Politics* (Cambridge: Cambridge University Press, 2024), 161.
10. Rosetta Thurman. "Nonprofits Don't Really Care About Diversity." *Stanford Social Innovation Review,* May 18, 2011. https://ssir.org/articles/entry/nonprofits_dont_really_care_about_diversity
11. Lily Zheng. "The Failure of the DEI-Industrial Complex." *Harvard Business Review,* December 1, 2022. https://hbr.org/2022/12/the-failure-of-the-dei-industrial-complex
12. Coleman Hughes. "Why Is TED Scared of Color Blindness?" Coleman's Corner, September 28, 2023. https://colemanhughes.substack.com/p/why-is-ted-scared-of-color-blindness
13. Jesse Singal. "Organizational Leaders Like Chris Anderson Should Stop Indulging Their Most Hysterical Employees." *Singal-Minded,* September 29, 2023. https://jessesingal.substack.com/p/organizational-leaders-like-chris

Chapter 2

1. In recent years, the Law Center has attracted a fair amount of controversy for who it puts on its hate watchlist. A number of individuals and organizations have complained that they were added to this list just because they are conservative or because they challenge progressive orthodoxy on a certain topic. For example, Maajid Nawaz successfully sued the organization for labeling him an anti-Muslim extremist, winning a $3 million settlement and an apology.
2. Nathan J. Robinson. "The Southern Poverty Law Center Is Everything That's Wrong With Liberalism." *Current Affairs,* March 26, 2019. https://www.currentaffairs.org/2019/03/the-southern-poverty-law-center-is-everything-thats-wrong-with-liberalism
3. "How the Southern Poverty Law Center Got Rich Fighting the Klan." *The Progressive,* July 1, 1988. https://progressive.org/magazine/how-the-southern-poverty-law-center-got-rich-fighting-the-klan/
4. Ben Schreckinger. "Has a Civil Rights Stalwart Lost Its Way?" *Politico,* July/August 2017. https://www.politico.com/magazine/story/2017/06/28/morris-dees-splc-trump-southern-poverty-law-center-215312/
5. Adeel Hassan, Karen Zraick, and Alan Blinder. "Morris Dees, a Co-Founder of the Southern Poverty Law Center, Is Ousted." *New York Times,* March 14, 2019. https://www.nytimes.com/2019/03/14/us/morris-dees-southern-poverty-law-center-fired.html
6. Bob Moser. "The Reckoning of Morris Dees and the Southern Poverty Law Center." *The New Yorker,* March 21, 2019. https://www.newyorker.com/news/news-desk/the-reckoning-of-morris-dees-and-the-southern-poverty-law-center
7. Matt Pearce. "Southern Poverty Law Center Fires Co-Founder Morris Dees Amid Employee Uproar." *Los Angeles Times,* March 14, 2019. https://www.latimes.com/nation/la-na-splc-morris-dees-20190314-story.html
8. Timothy Sandoval, "Sexual Harassment Is Widespread Problem for Fundraisers, Survey Shows." *Chronicle of Philanthropy,* April 5, 2018. https://www.philanthropy.com/article/sexual-harassment-is-widespread-problem-for-fundraisers-survey-shows/
9. "The Race to Lead Series." Building Movement Project. https://racetolead.org. Accessed October 18, 2024.
10. "#JustPay." Human Services Council. https://www.justpayny.org/facts-and-research. Accessed October 18, 2024.
11. Thomas B. Edsall. "Democrats Are Having a Purity-Test Problem at Exactly the Wrong Time." *New York Times,* June 29, 2022. https://www.nytimes.com/2022/06/29/opinion/progressive-nonprofits-philanthropy.html

12. Aaron Terrazas. "Glassdoor's 2024 Workplace Trends." Glassdoor, November 15, 2023. https://www.glassdoor.com/research/workplace-trends-2024#Trend1
13. All of the statistics in this section are taken from: Kristen Bialik and Richard Fry. "Millennial Life: How Young Adulthood Today Compares With Previous Generations." Pew Research Center, February 14, 2019. https://www.pewresearch.org/social-trends/2019/02/14/millennial-life-how-young-adulthood-today-compares-with-prior-generations-2/
14. "News: Unemployment Is at Its Lowest Level in 54 Years." US Department of Commerce, February 3, 2023. https://www.commerce.gov/news/blog/2023/02/news-unemployment-its-lowest-level-54-years
15. Darian Woods and Wailin Wong. "How to Measure Balance of Power Between Employers and Workers." NPR, May 12, 2023. https://www.npr.org/2023/05/12/1175893487/how-to-measure-balance-of-power-between-employers-and-workers
16. Jonathan Greig. "90% of Millennials and Gen-Z Do Not Want to Return to Full-Time Office Work Post-Pandemic." *ZDNet*, May 25, 2021. https://www.zdnet.com/article/90-of-millennials-gen-z-do-not-want-to-return-to-full-time-office-work-post-pandemic-report/
17. Victoria Rideout and S. Craig Watkins. "Millennials, Social Media, and Politics." Institute for Media Innovation, February 2019. https://moody.utexas.edu/sites/default/files/Millennials-Social-Media-Politics.pdf
18. Katherine Donlevy. "People Born in the '90s Not Recovering From Mental Health Issues as They Age: Study." *New York Post*, November 29, 2023. https://nypost.com/2023/11/29/lifestyle/each-generation-suffering-worse-mental-health-than-last-study/
19. Kim Parker, Nikki Graf, and Ruth Igielnik. "Generation Z Looks a Lot Like Millennials on Key Social and Political Issues." Pew Research Center, January 17, 2019. https://www.pewresearch.org/social-trends/2019/01/17/generation-z-looks-a-lot-like-millennials-on-key-social-and-political-issues/
20. "Rabbi David Wolpe: Harvard, Antisemitism, and Resilience." YouTube, March 18, 2024. https://www.youtube.com/watch?v=XpXTCIH06kc. Accessed October 18, 2024.
21. "The Millennial Economy." Economic Innovation Group. https://eig.org/millennial/#1473660719617-6a185bea-4da7. Accessed October 18, 2024.
22. Elizabeth Faber. "Millennial and Gen Z Employees Are Rejecting Assignments, Turning Down Offers, and Seeking Purpose. Here's What They Expect of Their Employers, According to Deloitte's Latest Survey." *Fortune*, July 6, 2023. https://fortune.com/2023/07/06/millennial-gen-z-employees-are-rejecting-assignments-turning-down-offers-and-seeking-purpose-they-expect-of-employers-according-to-deloittes-latest-survey/

23. Thomas Chatterton Williams (@thomaschattwill). "One of the less remarked upon features . . ." X, May 2, 2024. https://twitter.com/thomaschattwill/status/1786071581627666504. Accessed October 18, 2024.
24. Ryan Grim. "Elephant in the Zoom." *The Intercept*, June 13, 2022. https://theintercept.com/2022/06/13/progressive-organizing-infighting-callout-culture/
25. John Ellis. "A Reckless Age." *Political News Items*, February 18, 2024. https://substack.news-items.com/p/a-reckless-age?r=1t648&utm_campaign=post&utm_medium=email
26. Steve Kaagan and John Hagan. "Learning From an Intergenerational Blowup Over Social Justice." *Stanford Social Innovation Review*, January 4, 2024. https://ssir.org/articles/entry/an_intergenerational_social_justice_meltdown

Chapter 3

1. Robert B. Talisse. "The Polarization Dynamic." *Discourse*, January 26, 2021. https://www.discoursemagazine.com/p/the-polarization-dynamic
2. Ben Klutsey. "Too Much of a Good Thing." *Discourse*, November 6, 2020. https://www.discoursemagazine.com/p/too-much-of-a-good-thing
3. Carl Campanile. "Taxpayer-Funded Bronx Legal Aid Honcho Blasts Israel, 'US Empire' for 'Genocide.'" *New York Post*, June 1, 2021. https://nypost.com/2021/06/01/bronx-legal-aid-honcho-blasts-israel-us-empire-for-genocide/
4. Carl Campanile. "NYC Legal Aid Group Forced to Apologize, Pay $170K over Anti-Semitism Claim." *New York Post*, March 8, 2023. https://nypost.com/2023/03/08/bronx-defenders-apologize-settle-antisemitism-claim/
5. Santul Nerkar and Jonah E. Bromwich. "How the Israel-Hamas War Tore Apart Public Defenders in the Bronx." *New York Times*, December 14, 2023. https://www.nytimes.com/2023/12/14/nyregion/bronx-defenders-israel-gaza.html
6. "The Bronx Defenders Union: UAW Local 2325 Statement in Support of Palestinians." October 20, 2023. https://drive.google.com/file/d/15Hzyy_ufSJ9h8GjiYdg4eRKdGIUyikRE/view. Accessed October 18, 2024.
7. Cass R. Sunstein. "Conformity and the Dangers of Group Polarization." *Quillette*, May 17, 2019. https://quillette.com/2019/05/17/conformity-and-the-dangers-of-group-polarization/
8. "Americans' Views of the Israel-Hamas War." Pew Research Center. December 8, 2023. https://www.pewresearch.org/politics/2023/12/08/americans-views-of-the-israel-hamas-war/#:~:text=Currently%2C%2052%25%20say%20that%2C,two%2Dstate%20arrangement%20is%20possible.
9. "Will Social Justice Break Bronx Defenders?" Simple Justice, December 14, 2023. https://blog.simplejustice.us/2023/12/14/will-social-justice-break-bronx-defenders/

10. Theda Skocpol. "Associations Without Members." *The American Prospect,* December 19, 2001. https://prospect.org/power/associations-without-members/
11. David Callahan. "What Can Philanthropy Do to Curb Polarization?" *Inside Philanthropy,* June 14, 2022. https://www.insidephilanthropy.com/home/2022/6/14/a-conversation-with-steve-teles
12. Alexander C. Furnas and Timothy M. LaPira. "Political Elites Are More Supportive of Progressive Policies Than the Average Voter." Data for Progress, December 9, 2021. https://www.dataforprogress.org/blog/2021/12/9/political-elites-are-more-supportive-of-progressive-policies-than-the-average-voter
13. Dan Cardinali. "The Adaptive Challenge of Restoring Trust in Civil Society." *Stanford Social Innovation Review,* June 14, 2018. https://ssir.org/articles/entry/the_adaptive_challenge_of_restoring_trust_in_civil_society
14. "Joint Statement: College and University Trustees and Regents Must Join Peers in Committing to Institutional Neutrality." July 11, 2024. https://institutionalneutrality.org. Accessed October 18, 2024.

Chapter 4

1. "Focusing on What Works for Workplace Diversity." McKinsey & Company, April 7, 2017. https://www.mckinsey.com/featured-insights/gender-equality/focusing-on-what-works-for-workplace-diversity
2. Sarah Kessler. "DEI Goes Quiet." *New York Times,* January 13, 2024. https://www.nytimes.com/2024/01/13/business/dealbook/dei-goes-quiet.html
3. Matt Grossman and David A. Hopkins. *Polarized by Degrees: How the Diploma Divide and the Culture War Transformed American Politics* (Cambridge: Cambridge University Press, 2024), 220.
4. Greg Berman. "Diversity, Equity and Inclusion: What Do Nonprofit Leaders Really Think?" *New York Nonprofit Media,* December 5, 2022. https://www.nynmedia.com/opinion/2022/12/diversity-equity-and-inclusion-what-do-nonprofit-leaders-really-think/380442/
5. Suzanne Lucas. "How to Avoid a DEI Disaster Like the MS Society Just Had." *Inc.,* February 24, 2024. https://www.inc.com/suzanne-lucas/how-avoid-dei-disaster-ms-society.html
6. Christopher F. Rufo. "How DEI Corrupts America's Universities." *City Journal,* June 23, 2024. https://www.city-journal.org/article/how-dei-corrupts-americas-universities
7. Gregory Conti. "Why the Veep Picks Matter." *Compact,* August 16, 2024. https://www.compactmag.com/article/why-the-veep-picks-matter/

8. Andrew Lawrence. "Racist Dog Whistle: The Right Wing Has Weaponized 'DEI.'" *The Guardian*, April 21, 2024. https://www.theguardian.com/culture/2024/apr/21/dei-language-conservatives-baltimore
9. Tammi Rossman-Benjamin. "Why DEI Programs Can't Address Campus Antisemitism." *Sapir*, August 7, 2023. https://sapirjournal.org/antisemitism/2023/08/why-dei-programs-cant-address-campus-antisemitism/
10. Bari Weiss. "End DEI." *Tablet*, November 7, 2023. https://www.tabletmag.com/sections/news/articles/end-dei-bari-weiss-jews
11. Joseph Klein. "Call 'Affinity Groups' What They Are: Segregation." Foundation Against Intolerance & Racism, April 12, 2023. https://news.fairforall.org/p/call-racial-affinity-groups-what
12. Tema Okun. "White Supremacy Culture." https://www.whitesupremacyculture.info/uploads/4/3/5/7/43579015/okun_-_white_sup_culture.pdf. Accessed October 18, 2024.
13. "Tema Okun on Her Mythical Paper on White Supremacy." *The Intercept*, February 3, 2023. https://theintercept.com/2023/02/03/deconstructed-tema-okun-white-supremacy/
14. Robert Tracinski. "Where Progressives and the Alt-Right Meet." *The Bulwark*, July 21, 2020. https://www.thebulwark.com/p/where-progressives-and-the-alt-right-meet
15. Conor Friedersdorf. "'They Learn to Parrot What They Know They Are Supposed to Say.'" *The Atlantic*, May 17, 2021. https://www.theatlantic.com/ideas/archive/2021/05/true-inclusion-requires-viewpoint-diversity/618899/
16. Uri Berliner. "I've Been at NPR for 25 Years. Here's How We Lost America's Trust." *The Free Press*, April 9, 2024. https://www.thefp.com/p/npr-editor-how-npr-lost-americas-trust
17. Michael Shermer (@michaelshermer). "Helen Pluckrose explains how . . ." X. August 27, 2024. https://x.com/michaelshermer/status/1828543867366547842. Accessed October 18, 2024.
18. Elisabeth Lasch-Quinn. *Race Experts* (New York: W.W. Norton, 2001). xii–xvi.
19. Elizabeth Weingarten. "The Open Secret of What Works—and What Doesn't—for Diversity, Equity, and Inclusion." *Behavioral Scientist*, October 16, 2022. https://behavioralscientist.org/the-open-secret-of-what-works-and-what-doesnt-for-diversity-equity-and-inclusion/
20. Patricia G. Devine and Tory L. Ash. "Diversity Training Goals, Limitations, and Promise: A Review of the Multidisciplinary Literature." *Annual Review of Psychology*, March 14, 2022. https://www.ncbi.nlm.nih.gov/pmc/articles/PMC8919430/
21. Steve Lohr. "How a Diversity Initiative Changed Course With the Times." *New York Times*, January 22, 2024. https://www.nytimes.com/2024/01/22/business/diversity-oneten-black-employment.html

22. Greg Berman. "'We're Ignoring Our Common Values and Interests.'" *The Fulcrum*, September 24, 2024.
23. Yascha Mounk, *The Identity Trap* (New York: Penguin, 2023), 194.
24. Frank Dobbin and Alexandra Kalev. "Why Diversity Programs Fail." *Harvard Business Review*, July–August 2016. https://hbr.org/2016/07/why-diversity-programs-fail
25. David Brooks. "Universities Are Failing at Inclusion." *New York Times*, November 16, 2023. https://www.nytimes.com/2023/11/16/opinion/college-university-antisemitism-crt.html
26. Heather Templeton Dill et al. "We Disagree on Many Things but We Speak as One Voice in Support of Philanthropic Pluralism." *Chronicle of Philanthropy*, April 18, 2023. https://www.philanthropy.com/article/we-disagree-on-many-things-but-we-speak-with-one-voice-in-support-of-philanthropic-pluralism?utm_source=substack&utm_medium=email
27. Lauren Braithwaite. "The More You Know: Key Facts About Black Nonprofit Leadership." Candid, October 10, 2024. https://blog.candid.org/post/key-facts-on-nonprofit-black-leadership-candid-abfe/#:~:text=Based%20on%20data%20from%20nonprofits,or%20more%20Black%20board%20members.

Chapter 5

1. Yascha Mounk, *The Great Experiment: Why Diverse Democracies Fall Apart and How They Can Endure* (New York: Penguin Press, 2022), 253.
2. "About Maurice Mitchell." Working Families Party. https://workingfamilies.org/about-maurice-mitchell/. Accessed October 18, 2024.
3. Maurice Mitchell. "Building Resilient Organizations." The Forge, November 29, 2022. https://forgeorganizing.org/article/building-resilient-organizations
4. Daniel Goleman. "What Makes a Leader?" The Best of HBR, 1998. http://fs.ncaa.org/Docs/DIII/What%20Makes%20a%20Leader.pdf. Accessed October 18, 2024.
5. Daniel Goleman. "What Makes a Leader?" The Best of HBR, 1998. http://fs.ncaa.org/Docs/DIII/What%20Makes%20a%20Leader.pdf. Accessed October 18, 2024.
6. Asher J. Montgomery. "For Some Harvard Kennedy School Students, 'Crown Jewel' Leadership Class Leaves Emotional Scars." *The Harvard Crimson*, November 10, 2023. https://www.thecrimson.com/article/2023/11/10/harvard-kennedy-school-leadership-course/
7. Shankar Vedantam. "Lessons in Leadership: It's Not About You (It's About Them)." NPR, November 11, 2013. https://www.npr.org/2013/11/11/230841224/lessons-in-leadership-its-not-about-you-its-about-them

8. "Becoming an Adaptive Leader." *Lifelong Faith Journal,* Spring 2011. https://www.lifelongfaith.com/uploads/5/1/6/4/5164069/becoming_an_adaptive_leader.pdf. Accessed October 17, 2024.
9. "Robert K. Greenleaf, Servant-Leader." YouTube. https://www.youtube.com/watch?v=afOByZ8JlrE
10. Steve Inskeep and Lisa Weiner. "When Institutions Are Used As Stages, People Lose Trust, Book Argues." NPR, January 30, 2020. https://www.npr.org/2020/01/30/800922222/when-institutions-are-used-as-stages-people-lose-trust-book-argues. Accessed October 17, 2024.
11. Suzette Brooks Masters. "Philanthropy Needs to Own Up to Its Role in Fueling Polarization." *Chronicle of Philanthropy,* March 31, 2022. https://www.philanthropy.com/article/philanthropy-needs-to-own-up-to-its-role-in-fueling-polarization
12. Morgan Housel. *Same as Ever: A Guide to What Never Changes* (New York: Penguin 2023), 127.

Chapter 6

1. Justin McCarthy. "U.S. Approval for Labor Unions at Highest Point Since 1965." Gallup, August 30, 2022. https://news.gallup.com/poll/398303/approval-labor-unions-highest-point-1965.aspx
2. Jim Rendon. "Why Workers at Growing Numbers of Nonprofits Are Unionizing." AP, January 31, 2023. https://apnews.com/article/labor-unions-southern-poverty-law-center-business-race-and-ethnicity-7fd961c88c614db47db63ffcd80e084e
3. Julie Satow. "They Want to Change the World. They Would Also Like a Raise." *New York Times,* April 28, 2023. https://www.nytimes.com/2023/04/28/nyregion/nonprofits-unions.html
4. Julie Satow. "They Want to Change the World. They Would Also Like a Raise." *New York Times,* April 28, 2023. https://www.nytimes.com/2023/04/28/nyregion/nonprofits-unions.html
5. Greg Berman. "What Do Nonprofit Leaders Really Think About Unionization?" *New York Nonprofit Media,* May 2, 2022. https://www.nynmedia.com/opinion/2022/05/what-do-nonprofit-leaders-really-think-about-unionization/374270/
6. Vu Lee. "Our Default Organizational Decision-Making Model Is Flawed. Here's an Awesome Alternative!" Nonprofit AF, December 2, 2018. https://nonprofitaf.com/2018/12/our-default-organizational-decision-making-model-is-flawed-heres-an-awesome-alternative/
7. Tom Nixon. "Resolving the Awkward Paradox in Frederic Laloux's Reinventing Organisations." Medium, April 15, 2014. https://blog.maptio.

com/resolving-the-awkward-paradox-in-frederic-laloux-s-reinventing-organisations-f2031080ea02

8. Bob Morris. "Frederic Laloux: Part One of an Interview." bobmorris.biz, October 23, 2014. https://bobmorris.biz/frederic-laloux-part-1-of-an-interview-by-bob-morris
9. Nicole Wires. "Making Economic Democracy Work: How to Practice Shared Leadership." *Nonprofit Quarterly*, November 28, 2023. https://nonprofitquarterly.org/making-economic-democracy-work-how-to-practice-shared-leadership/
10. Mahmoud Farag. "The Rise and Fall of a Teal NGO." *Stanford Social Innovation Review*, April 10, 2017. https://ssir.org/articles/entry/the_rise_and_fall_of_a_teal_ngo
11. Faye Christoforo. "Want Democratic Leadership at Your Nonprofit? Here Are Some Dos and Don'ts." *Nonprofit Quarterly*, May 7, 2024. https://nonprofitquarterly.org/want-democratic-leadership-at-your-nonprofit-here-are-some-dos-and-donts/
12. Zachary Roth. "Making Participatory Budgeting Work: Experiences on the Front Lines." Brennan Center for Justice, August 23, 2022. https://www.brennancenter.org/our-work/analysis-opinion/making-participatory-budgeting-work-experiences-front-lines
13. Monica Marie Avery. "What I'm Learning: Drawing on Participatory Budgeting Principles to Experiment With Distributed Power." CompassPoint, July 26, 2023. https://www.compasspoint.org/blog/what-i'm-learning-drawing-participatory-budgeting-principles-experiment-distributed-power

Chapter 7

1. Eboo Patel. "A Nonprofit Mentoring Crisis Threatens the Future Leadership of the Field." *Chronicle of Philanthropy*, November 29, 2023. https://www.philanthropy.com/article/a-nonprofit-mentoring-crisis-threatens-future-leadership-of-the-field?sra=true
2. Ashleigh Webber. "Third of Employers Seeing More Employee Grievances." *Personnel Today*, February 1, 2023. https://www.personneltoday.com/hr/employee-grievances-rise-xperthr/
3. Stacey Lindsay. "In His New Book, Journalist Frank Bruni Shares How to Move Away From the 'Blame Game' and Toward THIS Hopeful Salvation." *Maria Shriver's Sunday Paper*, April 27, 2024. https://www.mariashriversundaypaper.com/frank-bruni-age-of-grievance/
4. "Ready to Lead? Next Generation Leaders Speak Out." https://www.compasspoint.org/sites/default/files/documents/521_readytolead2008.pdf. Accessed October 17, 2024.

5. Joan Garry. "Do You Need a Coach, a Mentor, or Both?" Joan Garry Consulting. https://www.joangarry.com/coach-mentor/. Accessed October 18, 2024.
6. Edwin P. Hollander. "Leadership and Social Exchange Processes." State University of New York at Buffalo, September 1976. https://apps.dtic.mil/sti/pdfs/ADA031224.pdf. Accessed October 17, 2024.
7. Adam Grant. "In the Company of Givers and Takers." *Harvard Business Review*, April 2013. https://hbr.org/2013/04/in-the-company-of-givers-and-takers
8. "Yuval Levin Explains the Importance of Institutional Trust and Reform." University of Maryland School of Public Policy, February 25, 2021. https://spp.umd.edu/news/yuval-levin-explains-importance-institutional-trust-and-reform. Accessed October 18, 2024.
9. Mark Nevins. "How to Make Mentoring Work Better." *Forbes*, March 30, 2023. https://www.forbes.com/sites/hillennevins/2023/03/30/how-to-be-a-better-mentee/
10. Mark Nevins. "How to Make Mentoring Work Better." *Forbes*, March 30, 2023. https://www.forbes.com/sites/hillennevins/2023/03/30/how-to-be-a-better-mentee/

Chapter 8

1. "Statement on Gaza/Palestine by People Who Are: PPFA Union Members, Former Employees, Current and Former Planned Parenthood Affiliate Employees, and Planned Parenthood Supporters and Donors." https://docs.google.com/forms/d/e/1FAIpQLScP5y1o_JQ3ofJFeEtAc9MqUGBWcuQlUyAOk5QraEZed8Ui7g/viewform?pli%3D1&sa=D&source=editors&ust=1704899590562673&usg=AOvVaw200wkZt7et1EuJASYo2ru1. Accessed October 19, 2024.
2. Sam Catanzaro. "Culver City's Wende Museum Looking to Expand to Include Housing for Homeless Artists." *Santa Monica Mirror*, November 19, 2021. https://smmirror.com/2021/11/culver-citys-wende-museum-looking-to-expand-to-include-housing-for-homeless-artists/
3. Geoff Dembicki. "Why 'Defunding the Police' Is Also an Environmental Issue." *Vice*, June 18, 2020. https://www.vice.com/en/article/why-defunding-the-police-is-also-an-environmental-issue/
4. Elizabeth Merritt. "In Praise of Mission Creep." American Alliance of Museums. June 15, 2002. https://www.aam-us.org/2022/06/15/in-praise-of-mission-creep/
5. Vu Le. "We Need to Rethink the Concept of 'Mission Creep.'" Nonprofit AF, August 22, 2021. https://nonprofitaf.com/2021/08/we-need-to-rethink-the-concept-of-mission-creep/
6. "Mission Creep: Nonprofit Kudzu." Successful Nonprofits, September 16, 2020. https://successfulnonprofits.com/pbpa-reverse-podcast/

7. Kim Jonker and William F. Meehan III. "Curbing Mission Creep." *Stanford Social Innovation Review,* Winter 2008. https://bpb-us-w2.wpmucdn.com/sites.cmc.edu/dist/1/6/files/2013/03/2008WI_casestudy_jonker_meehan.pdf
8. Jeremiah Johnson. "Against Activist Mission Creep." *Liberal Currents,* January 10, 2024. https://www.liberalcurrents.com/against-activist-mission-creep/
9. Matt Grossmann (@MattGrossmann). "Many of the staid organizations . . ." X. June 15, 2022. https://twitter.com/MattGrossmann/status/1537040688063426562. Accessed October 19, 2024.
10. Kim Jonker and William F. Meehan III. "Mission Matters Most." *Stanford Social Innovation Review,* February 19, 2014. https://ssir.org/articles/entry/mission_matters_most
11. John Tierney. "The March of Dimes Syndrome." *City Journal,* Spring 2004. https://www.city-journal.org/article/the-march-of-dimes-syndrome?utm_source=mailchimp&utm_medium=email&utm_campaign=cjdaily
12. Stephanie Strom. "Mission Accomplished, Nonprofits Go Out of Business." *New York Times,* April 1, 2011. https://www.nytimes.com/2011/04/02/business/02charity.html
13. Greg Berman. "Leader to Leader: Rich Leimsider." *New York Nonprofit Media,* December 10, 2022. https://www.nynmedia.com/personality/2022/12/leader-leader-rich-leimsider/380733/

Chapter 9

1. Jo Constantz. "CEOs Are Leaving Their Jobs in Record Numbers in What Is the Executive Suite Version of The Great Resignation." *Fortune,* October 19, 2023. https://fortune.com/2023/10/19/ceo-departures-highest-level-on-record-great-resignation/
2. Jim Rendon. "Large Numbers of Nonprofit Leaders Are Stepping Down—And the Competition to Find New Ones Is 'Fierce.'" *Chronicle of Philanthropy,* May 3, 2022. https://www.philanthropy.com/article/large-numbers-of-nonprofit-leaders-are-stepping-down-and-the-competition-to-find-new-ones-is-fierce?sra=true
3. Jim Rendon. "Large Numbers of Nonprofit Leaders Are Stepping Down—And the Competition to Find New Ones Is 'Fierce.'" *Chronicle of Philanthropy,* May 3, 2022. https://www.philanthropy.com/article/large-numbers-of-nonprofit-leaders-are-stepping-down-and-the-competition-to-find-new-ones-is-fierce?sra=true
4. Adrian Sargeant and Harriet Day. "A Study of Nonprofit Leadership in the US and Its Impending Crisis." Sustainable Philanthropy, 2018. https://concordleadershipgroup.com/!WakeUpCall_Report.pdf. Accessed October 19, 2024.

5. Gali Cooks and Eben Harrell. "Lessons from the Front Line for Nonprofit CEO Successions." *Stanford Social Innovation Review*, January 9, 2020. https://ssir.org/articles/entry/lessons_from_the_front_line_for_nonprofit_ceo_successions
6. Celine Coggins. "The Five Stages of Founder Transitions." *Stanford Social Innovation Review*, August 19, 2020. https://ssir.org/articles/entry/the_five_stages_of_founder_transitions
7. Jari Tuomola, Donald Yeh, and Katie Smith Milway. "Making Founder Successions Work." *Stanford Social Innovation Review*, Spring 2018. https://ssir.org/articles/entry/making_founder_successions_work#
8. "Leadership Transition in a Time of Turmoil: FLY Names a New CEO." Bridgespan Group. September 1, 2020. https://www.bridgespan.org/insights/leadership-transition-in-time-of-turmoil. Accessed October 19, 2024.
9. Frances Kunreuther and Sean Thomas-Breitfeld. "Fewer People Want to Lead Nonprofits. What's the Answer?" *Chronicle of Philanthropy*, January 26, 2024. https://www.philanthropy.com/article/fewer-people-want-to-lead-nonprofits-whats-the-answer?sra=true
10. Chanda Causer. "The Hollow Prize for Leaders of Color." *Stanford Social Innovation Review*, April 8, 2024. https://ssir.org/articles/entry/nonprofit-leadership-challenges-BIPOC-leaders
11. Nathan Glazer. "Is New York City Ungovernable?" *Commentary*, September 1961. https://www.commentary.org/articles/nathan-glazer-2/is-new-york-city-ungovernable/
12. Dana O'Donovan and Jarasa Kanak. "It's Time for Real Talk About Leadership Transitions." Deloitte, April 6, 2022. https://www2.deloitte.com/us/en/blog/monitor-institute-blog/2022/nonprofit-leadership-transitions.html
13. Jari Tuomola, Donald Yeh, and Katie Smith Milway. "Making Founder Successions Work." *Stanford Social Innovation Review*, Spring 2018. https://ssir.org/articles/entry/making_founder_successions_work#
14. Robert Greenleaf. Quotes. Goodreads. Accessed January 30, 2025. https://www.goodreads.com/author/quotes/105978.Robert_K_Greenleaf#:~:text=The%20servant%2Dleader%20is%20servant,influence%2C%20fame%2C%20or%20wealth.&text=Ego%20can't%20sleep.,It%20disempowers.

Conclusion

1. Jonathan Ireland. "The Nonprofit Industrial Complex and the Corruption of the American City." *American Affairs*, Summer 2024. https://americanaffairsjournal.org/2024/05/the-nonprofit-industrial-complex-and-the-corruption-of-the-american-city/?utm_source=substack&utm_medium=email

2. Garry Tan (@garrytan). "Nonprofits are bad . . ." X. June 29, 2024. https://x.com/garrytan/status/1807137610923708817. Accessed October 19, 2024.
3. Claire Dunning. "The Origins of the Nonprofit Industrial Complex." LPE Project, May 29, 2023. https://lpeproject.org/blog/the-origins-of-the-nonprofit-industrial-complex/
4. Melissa Chen (@MsMelChen). "There's a good case to be made . . ." X. April 18, 2024. https://twitter.com/MsMelChen/status/1781128815873261867. Accessed October 19, 2024.
5. David A. Fahrenthold. "Would a Group Opposed to Police Blow the Whistle on Its Founder?" *New York Times,* August 25, 2024. https://www.nytimes.com/2024/08/25/us/brandon-anderson-rahim-ai.html
6. Emily Steel. "A Pattern of Lavish Spending at a Leading L.G.B.T.Q Nonprofit." *New York Times,* August 1, 2024. https://www.nytimes.com/2024/08/01/business/glaad-ceo-spending.html
7. Alyce McFadden and Shayla Colon. "Charity Founder Embezzled Millions and Spent on Lavish Meals, U.S. Says." *New York Times,* June 11, 2024. https://www.nytimes.com/2024/06/11/nyregion/modest-needs-charity-keith-taylor.html
8. Nicholas Kulish. "After Raising $90 Million in 2020, Black Lives Matter Has $42 Million in Assets." *New York Times,* May 17, 2022. https://www.nytimes.com/2022/05/17/business/blm-black-lives-matter-finances.html
9. David A. Fahrenthold. "I Cover Nonprofits. Who Should I Investigate Next?" *New York Times,* March 21, 2022. https://www.nytimes.com/2022/03/21/reader-center/nonprofit-wrongdoing.html
10. "Ford Foundation and a Coalition of Nonprofits Announce Launch of Corporate Guide for Employee Listening." Ford Foundation, May 16, 2023. https://www.fordfoundation.org/news-and-stories/news-and-press/news/ford-foundation-and-a-coalition-of-nonprofits-announce-launch-of-corporate-guide-for-employee-listening/
11. Jeff Cain. "Big Philanthropy to the Rescue? Think Again." *Chronicle of Philanthropy,* April 1, 2024. https://www.philanthropy.com/commons/big-philanthropy-to-the-rescue-think-again?sra=true
12. Robert O'Neill. "Power and Accountability in Civil Society." Harvard Kennedy School, May 23, 2023. https://www.hks.harvard.edu/faculty-research/policy-topics/social-innovation-philanthropy/power-and-accountability-civil
13. To be sure, there are efforts underway to rethink nonprofit boards. But the most prominent of these initiatives tend to be focused on ensuring that nonprofits have more diverse members, including those with "lived experience."
14. Rachel Kleinfeld. "The Coming Attacks on Nonprofits." *Chronicle of Philanthropy,* April 1, 2024. https://www.philanthropy.com/commons/the-coming-attacks-on-nonprofits

15. Alnoor Ebrahim. "The Many Faces of Nonprofit Accountability." Harvard Business School, p. 27. https://www.hbs.edu/ris/Publication%20Files/10-069.pdf. Accessed October 19, 2024.
16. Laura Otten. "Self-Serving vs. Public Serving." The Nonprofit Center at La Salle University, November 6, 2020. https://www.lasallenonprofitcenter.org/understanding-nonprofit-relationships/
17. Elizabeth Weingarten. "The Open Secret of What Works—and What Doesn't—for Diversity, Equity, and Inclusion." *Behavioral Scientist*, October 16, 2022. https://behavioralscientist.org/the-open-secret-of-what-works-and-what-doesnt-for-diversity-equity-and-inclusion/
18. Robert O'Neill. "Power and Accountability in Civil Society." Harvard Kennedy School, May 23, 2023. https://www.hks.harvard.edu/faculty-research/policy-topics/social-innovation-philanthropy/power-and-accountability-civil
19. Benjamin Soskis. "The Shifting Landscape of American Generosity." The Generosity Commission, July 2024. https://www.thegenerositycommission.org/wp-content/uploads/2024/07/Generosity-Commission_Landscape-Analysis_072424_Final.pdf
20. Benjamin Soskis. "The Shifting Landscape of American Generosity." The Generosity Commission, July 2024. https://www.thegenerositycommission.org/wp-content/uploads/2024/07/Generosity-Commission_Landscape-Analysis_072424_Final.pdf
21. Michael Hartmann. "Philanthropy on the Defensive." *American Affairs*, April 5, 2022. https://americanaffairsjournal.org/2022/04/philanthropy-on-the-defensive/#_ednref15
22. Benjamin Soskis. "Charitable Cause Pluralism and Prescription in Historical Perspective." Urban Institute, October 2023. https://www.urban.org/sites/default/files/2023-10/Charitable%20Cause%20Pluralism%20and%20Prescription%20in%20Historical%20Perspective.pdf

Epilogue

1. "Second Wave Resistance." Welcome Stack, June 18, 2023. https://www.welcomestack.org/p/second-wave-resistance
2. ACLU (@ACLU). "BREAKING: The AP just called the 2024 presidential election for Trump . . ." X, November 6, 2024. Accessed November 23, 2024 at https://twitter.com/ACLU/status/1854143139855978883?ref_src=twsrc%5Etfw%7Ctwcamp%5Etweetembed%7Ctwterm%5E1854143139855978883%7Ctwgr%5E4410cd977a02f59316f2e0431a2542a144d75c9b%7Ctwcon%5Es1_&ref_url=https%3A%2F%2Fwww.commondreams.org%2Fnews%2Fthe-resistance-to-a-new-trump

3. Conor Friedersdorf. "The Case for Treating Trump Like a Normal President." *The Atlantic*, November 8, 2024. https://www.theatlantic.com/politics/archive/2024/11/trump-normal-popular-vote/680578/
4. Daniel Stid. "Funding the Resistance Is Not a Winning Strategy. Here's What Is." *Chronicle of Philanthropy*, November 7, 2024. https://www.philanthropy.com/commons/trump-resistance-funding?oref=nyn_firstread_nl&utm_source=Sailthru&utm_medium=email&utm_campaign=NYN%20First%20Read%20-%20November%208%2C%202024&utm_term=newsletter_nyn_firstread
5. Yascha Mounk. "How Not to Resist Donald Trump." *Persuasion*, January 20, 2025. https://www.persuasion.community/p/how-not-to-resist-donald-trump
6. Cory J. Clark et al. "Even When Ideologies Align, People Distrust Politicized Institutions." Unpublished paper. Available at: https://osf.io/preprints/psyarxiv/sfubr. Accessed on November 9, 2024.
7. Jordan Heller. "The Free-Speech War Inside the ACLU." *New York*, January 17, 2025. https://nymag.com/intelligencer/article/the-free-speech-war-inside-the-aclu.html

INDEX

For the benefit of digital users, indexed terms that span two pages (e.g., 52–53) may, on occasion, appear on only one of those pages.

accountability
  challenges of, 161
  and corrupt practices, 162
  evaluating relevance, 140–142
  focusing on mission, 170–171
  government funding, 166–167
  and pressure to be "transparent," 115
  public, importance, 169
  responsibility to the public, 162, 170
  role of boards, 50, 167
  role of donors, 165–167
  role of staff, 164
  role of the media, 163
  and tax-exempt status, 162–164
  TED Talk example, 31–32
  using metrics for, 106
ACLU (American Civil Liberties Union), 178–180
activism
  cultural conservatism, 75
  and internal disruption, 47–49
  and mission creep, 137–138, 140
adaptability, 15, 18, 84, 88–89, 172–173
affirmative action, 21–22, 72, 83–84
Allen, Woody, 36
Allison, Graham T., 99
American Affairs, on nonprofit failures, 160
American Alliance for Equal Rights, 83–84
Anderson, Chris, 6, 22–23, 31, 32–33
antisemitism, 24, 57–58, 76
Ash, Tory, 81–82
associations, public, 3–4, 16, 54–55, 63, 166, 176, 182
Atlantic, article about intern attitudes, 47–48
Avery, Marie, 114

Baby Boom generation, 42–43
Barasch, Amy, 126
Berliner, Uri, 76
best practices, 82, 169
Black Americans
  efforts of nonprofits to hire, 83
  positive impacts of DEI initiatives, 88–89
Black CEOs
  parallels with Black city mayors, 153–154
  special challenges faced by, 153
Black Lives Matter, 24–25, 30, 35, 66, 67, 71
Black Lives Matter Global Network Foundation, 162
'Black@TED' group, 22
Blum, Edward, 83–84

boards
  expectations for, 154–155
  and focusing on mission, 170
  role in accountability, 50, 167
  role in CEO transitions, 154–155
Bouie, Jamelle, 32
Bowling Alone (Putnam), 63
Brandel, Gayle, 147
Bratton, Bill, 52
Brazil, participatory budgeting in, 113–114
Bridgespan Group
  "best practices" guidelines, 169
  successful leadership transitions, 151, 158
Bronx Defenders, discrimination lawsuit against, 56–59
Brooks, David, 87
Bruni, Frank, 121
Bryan, Courtney, 114, 144
budgeting, participatory, 113–115
Buffet, Peter, 10
Buffet, Warren, 137
Building Movement Project, 40, 152–153
"Building Resilient Organizations" (Mitchell), 94–95
The Bulwark, article on definitions of white supremacy culture, 76

Cain, Jeff, 165
"A Case for Color Blindness" (Hughes), 21
Causer, Chanda, 153
Cave, Nick, 19
Center for Court Innovation
  collaborative policing initiative, 52–53
  growth and leadership needs, 144–145
  innovation fund, 114
  leadership decisions, 107, 144, 146–147
  political atmosphere, 53–54
  renaming as Center for Justice Innovation, 114, 144
Center for New Liberalism, 137–138
Center for the Future of Museums, 135
CEO transition process. *See also* leadership/stewardship
  bad transitions, 146–147
  cutting ties gradually, 151–152
  deciding to leave, 144–145, 148–149
  ego/self-regard, 149–150, 158
  and finding another job, 150–151
  growing disinterest in CEO positions, 152–153
  impacts on staff and organization, 145–146, 150–151
  knowing when it's time to go, 172–173
  personal financial needs, 42–43, 151
  role of boards, 155
  role of exiting leaders, 156–158
  role of funders, 155–156
  role of incoming leaders, 156
  role of nonprofits, 101
  role of staff, 156
  search process, 145–146
  succession plans, 147–149
  transition process, 145, 147
CEOs. *See also* leadership/stewardship
Chen, Melissa, critique of nonprofits, 161
Chronicle of Philanthropy
  on CEO turnover, 147
  and the "Great Resignation," 147
  Patel's column in, 120
  on philanthropic pluralism, 87–88
Civil Rights Act, 1964, Title VII, 83
Coggins, Celine, 150
collective intelligence concept, 111–113
Collier, John, 108
color-blind policies. *See* race conscious policymaking
Compact magazine, on cultural conservatism, 75
CompassPoint, participatory budgeting at, 114
Conformity: The Power of Social Influences (Sunstein), 59–60
conservatives, conservative voters, critiques of the nonprofit sector, 11–14
Coro Leadership Center fellowship program, 35
Covid-19 pandemic, 24–25, 44, 45–46, 147
criminal justice reform, 35–36, 145
culture wars, 16, 29, 79, 138, 164, 176, 183
Cumberbatch, Shannon, 57–58
Cynical Theories (Pluckrose), 76

Danube Institute, 11
Daum, Robert, 142
de Blasio, Bill, 52
deBoer, Freddie, 7–8
decision making, complexity, 117
decision-making
  challenges of, 104
  democratic, value of embracing, 68
  democratizing, cautions about, 115–117
  increasing staff voice in, 113–115
  and the need for diversity, 54
Dees, Morris, 37–39
"DEI Goes Quiet" (*New York Times*), 72
DEI initiatives
  affinity groups, 76
  beneficial aspects, 73, 83
  challenges to, 72–79, 83–84
  changing branding of, 85–86
  and cultural conservatism, 75
  effective, 171–172
  and the "firing" of Itkoff, 74–75
  hiring/promotion policy changes, 72
  indirect approaches, 86
  intergroup contact approaches, 85–86
  investments in, 30
  ongoing investments in, 82
  pluralism and, 87–88
  public policy agendas, 71, 96
DEI-industrial complex, 30, 161
democracy. *See* associations, public; membership associations
Democracy in America (Tocqueville), emphasis on "public associations" in, 3–4
Democratic Party, 12–13, 181
Devine, Patricia, 81–82
direct service organizations, 135
discipline, organizational, importance, 104–105, 132, 161, 183
"disease of more," 133–134. *See also* mission creep
distrust of civic institutions/public sector, 15, 30, 46–47, 101, 175, 181, 182
diversity, equity, and inclusion (DEI) initiatives. *See* DEI initiatives
diversity training
  ambivalence about, 69–71
  evaluating effectiveness, 81–82
  importance of mentoring for, 128–129
  Lasch-Quinn's critique, 79–80
"Diversity Training Goals, Limitations, and Promise: A Review of the Multidisciplinary Literature" (Devine and Ash), 81–82
Do Good Institute (University of Maryland), 175
Dobbin, Frank, 86–87, 172
Dobbs v. Jackson, 2022, 66
donors. *See* funding; philanthropy
Dunning, Claire, 161, 166–167

Ebrahim, Alnoor, 169
Egan, Margaret, 48
Eisenhower, Dwight, 8
Ellenbogen, Amy, 123, 127–128
Emotional Intelligence: Why It Can Matter More than IQ (Goleman), 98–99
emotional intelligence/empathy, 98–99
employees. *See* staff/staffing
equity, 69–70, 85. *See also* DEI initiatives
executive coaches, 157
executives. *See* CEOs; leadership/stewardship

Fahrenthold, David, 163
failure, learning from, 100, 135
"The Failure of the DEI-Industrial Complex" (*Harvard Business Review*), 30
fake engagement, 115
Fearless Fund, lawsuit against, 83–84
feedback
  instant, 96
  meaningful, importance, 120, 128, 129–130
  risks of, 120
  from staff, 53, 114–115, 145–146
Feinblatt, John, 119
Financial Times, on critiques of young staff, 49

flexibility, 18, 29–31, 98, 99–100, 103–104
Floyd, George, 66, 71
Ford Foundation, 11–12, 164
Foster, Jodie, 27
Foundation Against Intolerance and Racism, 76, 85
Foundation for Individual Rights and Expression, 67
Foxx, Virginia, investigation into Bronx Defenders union, 58
The Free Press
  callout of NPR for liberal bias, 76
  and the Coleman Hughes color-blind controversy, 32
Friedersdorf, Conor, 180
funding. *See also* philanthropy
  focus on projects *vs.* operations, 134
  funder stipulations, 9
  government funding, 9, 25–26, 166–167, 179
  grant requirements, 9
  influence on nonprofit performance, 9, 39, 57
  and mission creep, 134
  requirements of funding sources, 59–60
  role in accountability, 165–167
  short funding cycles, 134
Furnas, Alexander C., 64

Ganesh, Janan, 49
Gannon Christa, 152
Ganz, Marshall, 166
Gates, Bill, 126–127
Gaza, war in, 24–25, 58, 66–67, 135, 139–140. *See also* Bronx Defenders; mission creep
Generations (Twenge), 27–28
Generation Z
  comfort with digital environments, 44–46
  distrust of nonprofits, 15
  inflexibility, 36
  and staffing challenges, 27, 46–47, 52, 98
  workplace challenges
generosity, and effective mentoring, 126–128
Getting to Diversity (Dobbin and Kalev), 81, 86–87, 172
Giridharadas, Anand, 10
Giuliani, Rudy, 56
GLAAD
  mentoring experience at, 123
  misuse of funds at, 162
Glasser, Ira, 181–182
Glazer, Nathan, 153–154
Goldenburg, Dolph, 136
Goldman, Beth, on entrenched leadership, 148–149
Goleman, Daniel, on interpersonal skills needed by leaders, 98–99
government funding. *See* funding
The Great Experiment: Why Diverse Democracies Fall Apart and How They Can Endure (Mounk), 93, 181
Greenfield, Scott, 61
Greenleaf, Robert K., 100–101, 158
grievance culture, 120–122
Grim, Ryan, 48
Grossmann, Matt, 29, 138
The Guardian, on DEI as a "dog whistle" among cultural conservatives, 75

Hagan, John, 50
Hannah-Jones, Nikole, 182
Harris, Kamala, 182
Harris, Monica, 81
Harvard University
  affirmative action cases, 72, 76, 83–84
  endowment, 17
Heifetz, Ronald, 99
Heritage Foundation, Project 2025, 12
Herman, Susan, 52
Heterodox Academy, 67
Hollander, Edwin P., 125–126
Hopkins, David A., 29
Housel, Morgan, 103
Hughes, Coleman, 21–22, 31–32
human service providers, 17
humility, 100–101, 103–104
Huxley, Aldous, 86

INDEX

identity politics, 41, 72–73, 76, 85. *See also* DEI initiatives
The Identity Trap (Mounk), 85
impacts, 67–68
impacts, prioritizing, 64–68
INCITE! 8–9
innovation fund, 114
institutional memory, 146
institutional neutrality, 67
Interfaith America, 120
Internal Revenue Service
  expressed concerns about nonprofits, 168–169
  IRS Form 990, 163–164
  prohibition against involvement in electoral politics, 29
  tax-exempt status, 17, 162, 163–164
Ireland, Jonathan, 160
Itkoff, Fran, 5–7, 74–75

Johnson, Jeremiah, 137–138
Jonas, Debbie, 57–58
Jones, Alethia, 109
Jonker, Kim, 137, 139
Judis, John B., 12–13

Kaagan, Steve, 50
Kalev, Alexandra, 81, 86–87, 172
Kalven Report (University of Chicago), 139–140
Kanok, Jarasa, 156–157
Kennedy School of Government, adaptive leadership concept, 99
Kerr, Liam, 178
King, Martin Luther Jr., 21
Knight, Ali, 152

Laloux, Frederic, 111–113
LaPira, Tim, 64
Lasch-Quinn, Elisabeth, 79–80
Le, Vu, 110, 136
leadership/stewardship. *See also* accountability; CEO transition process; mentoring; staff/staffing
  adaptation skills, 107
  addressing polarization, 95
  and asking for advice, 97
  attention to diversity/equity, 40, 54, 69–70, 73, 88–89, 153–155
  business model of management, 106
  complaints about junior staffers, 49
  day-to-day management, 53
  decision making, 53, 104, 113–115, 117
  debunking myths about, 129
  demand for leaders of color, 147
  demonstrating trustworthiness, 20, 129
  despotic CEOs, 108–109
  emotional intelligence, 98–99
  engaging democratic decision-making, 68
  finding a middle ground, 34, 111, 182–183
  flexibility, 99–100
  growing "stale," 105, 148–149
  humility, 100–101
  and leaders of color, 153–155
  as leadership model, 97
  long-term thinking, 102–103
  need for patience, 95–96
  principle challenges faced by, 31
  under promising, 115
  providing access to real-life information, 127
  and rational optimism, 103
  resistance to unionization, 109–110
  role in nonprofit success, 173–174
  as a sacred trust/responsibility, 97
  sexual harassment charges, 40
  sublimating personal goals to needs of the organization, 97
  and top-down management approaches, 110
  "tough-love," corporate approaches, 96–97
left-wing ideology, and inflexibility, 36
Leimsider, Rich, 142–143, 153
Leonard, Dutch, 173, 175–176
Levin, Yuval, 101, 129
Lind, Michael, 13
long-term thinking, 102–103, 182
Los Angeles Lakers, 133–134
Los Angeles Times, on the SPLC, 39

loyalty, 55
loyalty, staff, 18, 45, 55, 124, 158

March of Dimes syndrome, 141–142
Masters, Suzette Brooks, 102–103
McSwain, Sharyanne, 147
#MeToo, 24–25
Meehan, William F., 137, 139
meetings, as a burden, 115
membership associations. *See* associations, public
mentoring. *See also* leadership/stewardship
  ad hoc approaches, 122–123
  bridging differences, 124
  formal leadership development programs, 122
  generosity, 126–128
  importance, 172
  mentorship experiences, 94–96, 123
  providing meaningful feedback, 120
  relationships underlying, 118
  role of the mentee, 129–130
  and self-interest, 118
  trust/reciprocity and, 124–126
Merritt, Elizabeth, 135
Messinger, Ruth, 149
microaggressions, 30, 41, 104
middle path, embracing, 96, 111
Millennial generation
  characteristics, 43–44
  comfort with digital environments, 44–46
  generalized anxiety, 47
  inflexibility, 36
  need for emotional intelligence, 98
  reshaping of workplace by, 27, 44, 45–46
  and staffing challenges, 46–48
mission creep
  in advocacy organizations, 137–138
  avoiding, 59, 104–105
  core competencies *vs.*, 137
  and the desire to be helpful, 135
  and the desire to do the right thing, 135
  and the "disease of more," 134
  examples in mission statements, 133
  funding-related factors, 134
  ideological *vs.* practical goals, 62
  kudzu analogy, 136
  and overly broad mission statements, 139
mission statements
  benefits of, 132–133, 136
  buzz words in, 65–66
  and changing to stay relevant, 140–142
  critiques of, 131–132
  and focus on public accountability, 170–171
  as focused and narrow, 132
  overpromising in, 133
  tightening and limiting, 139
  well-honed, characteristics, 139
Mitchell, Maurice, 94–95
Modest Needs, 162
Moser, Bob, 39
Mounk, Yascha, 85, 93, 181
Moynihan, Daniel Patrick, 176
Murthy, Vivek H., 45–46
museums, 5–6, 76, 133, 135, 137

National Museum of African American History and Culture, 76
National Public Radio (NPR), 76
Neighbors in Action, 123
Nevins, Mark, 130
New America think tank, 13
The New Jim Crow, 35
New York City
  Bronx Defenders, 56
  cost of living, 40
  nonprofits in economy of, 6
  2013 mayoral race, 52
New York Post, on the Bronx Defenders, 58
New York Times
  Brooks on pluralism, 87
  Bruni on age of grievance, 122
  "DEI Goes Quiet," 72
  focus on nonprofit corruption, 163
  on Justine Olderman, 58
  references to nonprofits in, 5–7
The New Yorker, Moser article on Dees, 39
Nonprofit Democracy Network, 112
"The Nonprofit Industrial Complex and the Corruption of the American City" (Ireland), 160

"A Nonprofit Mentoring Crisis Threatens Future Leadership of the Field" (Patel), 120
Nonprofit Professional Employees Union, 107–108
nonprofits/nonprofit sector
  criticisms of, 8–10, 15, 16, 26, 29–30, 106, 153–154, 160–161, 168–169
  distrust of, 14–15, 65, 101, 175–176, 182–183
  impact of Trump's election, 177–180
  importance and value, 3–4, 173, 174–176
  intergenerational conflict, 47–48
  long-term perspectives, 102–103
  monoculture in, 61
  need for reinvention, 134, 180
  numbers of, 4
  political atmosphere within, 54, 66
  as primarily left-leaning, 11–14, 26
  public disinterest in, 35–36
  racial disparities, 107–108
  range of functions, 4
  sexual harassment, 40
  wage inequality, 40

Obama administration, 168–169
O'Donovan, Dana, 156–157
Okun, Tema, 76
Olderman, Justine, 57–59
OneTen organization, 84
"Organizational Leaders like Chris Anderson Should Stop Indulging Their Most Hysterical Employees" (Singal), 33
organizational structure
  adapting to changing needs, 133
  collective intelligence approach, 111–113
  hierarchical, top-down management, 110
  innovation fund example, 114
  participatory budgeting, 113–114
  worker self-directed nonprofit, 112–113
O'Sullivan's First Law/John O'Sullivan, 11–12
Out2Play, 142
Overdoing Democracy: Why We Must Put Politics in Its Place (Talisse), 54–55
participatory budgeting, 113–114
Patel, Eboo, 120, 128
performing arts, role of nonprofits in, 5
philanthropy, private. *See also* funding
  debates about, 165–166
  dependence on, 25–26
  and the donor class, 166
  philanthropic colonialism concept, 10
  trickle-down philosophy, 165
Planned Parenthood, 133
Pluckrose, Helen, 76
"Pluralism and the Independent Sector" (Moynihan), 176
pluralism initiatives, 87–88
polarization, 28–30, 54–55, 61–63, 65, 168–169
Polarized by Degrees (Grossman and Hopkins), 29
policing, 52
Politico, SPLC article, 38
politicization, 13, 28–29, 54, 62–66, 139–140, 181
pop-up nonprofit, 142
power sharing, 113–114
productivity, 106
progressive ideology
  among young staff, 36, 53, 61
  conservative challenges, 179
  and mission creep, 135
  pressure to embrace, 135, 181–182
  and reform needs, 26
  and workplace disruption, 49–50, 94–95
PSLF.nyc, 142–143
Public Service Loan Forgiveness program, 142
Putnam, Robert, 63

race conscious policymaking, 21–22, 31, 35–36, 73, 83–84, 172
Race Experts: How Racial Etiquette, Sensitivity Training and New Age Therapy Hijacked the Civil Rights Revolution (Lasch-Quinn), 79–80
racial affinity groups, 76
Raheem AI, misuse of funds by, 162
Rainier Valley Corps, Seattle, 111

Ramone, Phil, 130
rational optimism, 103
Reagan, Ronald, 182
regulations, state and local, 163–164
Reinventing Organizations (Laloux), 134–135
The Revolution Will Not Be Funded: Beyond the Non-Profit Industrial Complex (INCITE!), 8
Riley, Pat, 133–134
Rossman-Benjamin, Tammi, 76
Rufo, Christopher, 72–73, 75

Salamon, Lester, 4–5
Same as Ever: A Guide to What Never Changes, (Housel), 103
"The Servant as Leader" (Greenleaf), 101
servant leadership, 101, 126–128, 158
sexual harassment, 40
short-term thinking, 102
shutting down, decisions about, 142
Singal, Jesse, 33
Sojourner, Aaron, 44
Soskis, Benjamin, 174–175
Southern Poverty Law Center (SPLC), 37–39
staff/staffing
  appeal of unions, 107–109
  challenges to leaders, 40, 47–48
  disruptive political atmosphere, 54
  domination by professionals, 63
  effects of polarization, 29–31, 41, 53–56
  efforts to diversify, 30, 54, 73, 83
  employee expectations, 24, 27–28, 46, 48, 98, 115, 120
  and fake engagement, 115
  grievance culture, 121
  increasing staff voices, 113–115
  limiting organizational power of, 170
  Millennial/Gem Z anxiety, 47–48
  role in accountability, 164
  staffing/staff, role in CEO transition process, 156
Stanford Social Innovation Review
  Causer article about Black executive directors, 153
  Jonker and Meehan article on preventing mission creep, 137
  Kaagan and Hagen article about "overreach," 50
  on white dominance of nonprofits, 30
The State of Nonprofit America (Salamon), 4–5
stewardship. *See* leadership/stewardship
Stid, Daniel, 180
"Stop Terror-Financing and Tax Penalties on American Hostages Act" Act, 5–6, 179
Students for Fair Admissions v. Harvard, 83
Successful Nonprofits podcast, 136
succession plans, 147–149. *See also* CEO transition process
Sunrise Movement, 133
Sunstein, Cass, 59–60
Supreme Court, DEI-related rulings, 72, 83–84
Sustainable Economies Law Center, Oakland, CA, 112–113

Talisse, Robert, 54–55
Tan, Garry, 161
tax-exempt status. *See* Internal Revenue Service
Teach Plus, 150
technological change, 27–28
TED Foundation/TED Talks
  accountability, 31–33
  'Black@TED' group, 22
  Coleman Hughes' talk, 21–22, 31
  leadership challenges, 22–23
Teixeira, Ruy, 12–13
Teles, Steven, domination of nonprofits by professionals, 63
A Time to Build (Levin), 101
Tocqueville, Alexis de, 8–9
Tracinski, Robert, 76
transparency, pressure for, 17, 47, 115
Trilling, Diana, 13
Trump, Donald, Trump administration
  anti-immigration policies, 102–103
  election of, impacts on nonprofits, 17, 177–179
  opposition to DEI initiatives, 72, 88

resisting policies of, 46, 177–179
support for, 178, 181
trust
and effective leadership, 98–99
and effective mentoring, 122, 124–125
public, importance, 20, 52–53, 65, 101, 104, 128–129
Twenge, Jean, 27–28

Ukraine War, 66
unions
appeal to nonprofit workers, 108–110
potential impacts of unionization, 24–25
increasing public approval for, 107
leadership concerns about, 109–110
Nonprofit Professional Employees Union, 107–108

Vance, J.D., 169, 179
viewpoint diversity, 76
Vital City, 146
volunteerism, decline in, 174–175

wage inequality, 40
Wales, Nicole, 111–113
Washington, George, 173
Watler, Chris, 153
Weiss, Barry, 76
Wende Museum, Culver City, CA, 133
Where Have All the Democrats Gone? (Judis and Teixeira), 12–13
white supremacy culture, 76
Williams, Thomas Chatterton, 47–48
Winners Take All: The Elite Charade of Changing the World (Giridharadas), 10
"wokeness," 13. *See also* polarization; politicization
Women's Prison Association, 48
worker self-directed nonprofits, 112–113

Youth on Boards, Action on Climate (YOB), 50